EYE ON THE BOTTOM LINE

ON THE GO

DRAWBRIDGE™

EYE ON THE BOTTOM LINE

Figuring Out the World of Figures

ON THE GO

ANIL LAMBA

HARPER BUSINESS

An Imprint of HarperCollins *Publishers*

First published in India in 2021 by Harper Business
An imprint of HarperCollins *Publishers India*
A-75, Sector 57, Noida, Uttar Pradesh 201301, India
www.harpercollins.co.in

2 4 6 8 10 9 7 5 3 1

P-ISBN: 978-93-5357-963-0
E-ISBN: 978-93-5357-964-7

Typeset in 9.5/11.5 TitilliumText25L at
Manipal Technology Ltd, Manipal

Printed and bound at
Thomson Press (India) Ltd

Disclaimer

To my fellow finance professionals for their contribution in making financially intelligent decisions and making businesses stable, profitable and sustainable.

Preface

Eye on the Bottom Line was written to complete the topics that were left out in ***Romancing the Balance Sheet***, and, in that sense, can be its sequel.

Being a ready reference of sorts, I had introduced a condensed edition of ***RTBS*** a while back in response to the feedback from people who were interested in bringing the book along on their travels, as well as those who couldn't muster the time to go through voluminous content.

This edition has received an extremely encouraging response, with readers having positive things to say about both the concise content as well as the compact, easy-to-carry size.

All arguments in favour of bringing out the travel edition of ***RTBS*** apply to ***Eye on the Bottom Line*** too.

I'm happy to bring to you ***Eye on the Bottom Line – On the Go,*** a lighter version of the original book.

With both books now available in travel editions, almost all the topics needed to practise good finance management will be ready at hand.

I await your views at
anil@lamconschool.com.

Anil Lamba

January 2021

Contents

PART I | RECAP

CHAPTER 1 Key Messages from Romancing the Balance Sheet

1. A non-finance person is an oxymoron

Finance management is the ability to take financially intelligent decisions.

Every action of every individual has either a positive or a negative impact on the organization's bottom line.

Profit is the cumulative result of the actions of every single individual within an organization.

There are persons within each business whose actions add to the bottom line and there are others who take away from it.

When the actions of those who are strengthening the bottom line are stronger than those who are hurting it, the net result is profit. If it is vice versa, the result is a loss.

Can you imagine an organization where every individual consciously takes only those actions by which the bottom line becomes stronger – what an amazing organization it would be!

There are non-accounting persons but there are no non-finance persons.

2. There is no connection between profit and money

It is possible for a business to make lots of profit and have no money. It is equally possible that it has a large bank balance and still does not make a profit.

Business is all about making profit. But there is no pleasure in making profit if at the end of the month there is no money to pay salaries.

Successful enterprises stand on two pillars:

i. Ability to generate profit

*ii. **Ability to effectively manage cash flows***

The responsibility for keeping both these pillars strong rests on the shoulders of those who often call themselves 'non-finance' persons – those in charge of procurement and production and sales and all the other key functions within any business.

Profits not accompanied by cash can be seriously detrimental for an organization's health.

3. Money spent is not an expense, money consumed is

A Profit & Loss Account and a Balance Sheet are the two key financial statements made by every organization.

The former reveals expenses and incomes and the latter liabilities and assets.

Since these two statements, between them, summarize everything that has happened over a certain period, it holds to reason that every transaction that takes place can eventually be classified as one of these four types.

This then gives us an insight into not only reading but also the making of these statements.

If one wishes to learn how to make a Profit & Loss Account and a Balance Sheet then all one has to do is to look at the transaction the moment it takes place and, bypassing the entire accounting system, transfer it straightaway into one of these four quadrants and the statements would be ready.

It can be as easy as that.

(This has been explained in greater detail later in the book.)

In fact, the job becomes twice as easy when one realizes that not only are there merely four options under which each transaction can be categorized, but, broadly speaking, all transactions can be broken up into those that bring money in and those that take it away.

Incomes and liabilities involve a cash inflow and expenses and assets an outflow.

One now realizes that it is no longer necessary to choose out of these four options. If the transaction involves an inflow, one needs to choose between income and liability. And if money has been spent, the choice is between expense and asset.

When money spent should be classified as income and when it should be called a liability is relatively easy to figure out. But whether the cash outflow has resulted in an expense or an asset can sometimes be confusing.

Here, the ultimate test is that of consumption.

- **Money spent on items that get entirely consumed before the date of making the Balance Sheet are called expenses.**
- **Money spent on items that are not consumed at all on the date of making the Balance Sheet are called assets.**
- **Money spent on items that are partially consumed and on the date of making the Balance Sheet are partially not consumed, to the extent consumed are called expenses and to the extent not consumed are called assets.**

A pertinent example to illustrate this is of raw material. The portion of raw material purchased that gets consumed is shown as an expense and the portion lying in the warehouse on the date of preparing the Balance Sheet appears as inventory on the assets' side of the Balance Sheet.

4. The role of expenses is to enable recovery

Another way of understanding whether money spent is an expense or whether it should be classified as an asset is to understand the role of each.

Both expenses and assets result in a cash outflow. But what happens when the money spent is shown as an expense? Expenses result in the reduction of profit.

Conversely, what happens when money spent is shown as an asset? The money has gone out, but the profit remains intact.

Expenses are opportunities to recover.

Based on this logic, when should money spent be called an expense and when should it be called an asset?

Since expenses enable recovery, all the money that an organization spends which it also wishes to recover should be called expenses. And only the money that it spends and does not wish to recover should be called assets.

But this doesn't make sense. Because if you ask any business person which money he would like to recover, what answer do you think you will get? The business person will obviously say that he doesn't spend any money that he doesn't wish to recover. He would like to recover all the money spent.

Each penny spent by a business entity needs to be recovered, whether towards the payment of salaries or the acquisition of a building.

And if expenses mean recovery, then as per this logic the entire money spent should be classified as expenses and there should be no assets.

Incidentally, this is the correct answer. All the money spent has to be recovered for an organization to make profit in the real sense.

So the question is not *whether* it wishes to recover, but *when* it wishes to recover the money spent.

There is money spent on certain items which if spent today, must also be recovered today. Such items are called expenses and are shown on the Profit & Loss Account.

There is money spent on other items which, of course, needs to be recovered, but you realize that there's no hurry to do so. You don't mind if you recover these over an extended period of time.

When you are willing to stagger the recovery, such items are temporarily called assets and shown as such on the Balance Sheet. And each installment of recovery is called depreciation, which gets recorded as an expense.

A Balance Sheet is like a warehouse where you store items till they get transferred to the Profit & Loss Account.

What needs to be understood is that the ultimate destination for every penny spent is the expenses' side of the Profit & Loss Account.

Nirvana is only attained when that happens.

5. Understanding the cost of capital

The first thing a business owner must understand and appreciate is that no money is free. Every penny invested in business has a cost, including the owners' money.

The owners' money not only has a cost, but it is the costliest source of money available.

The average cost of capital in most organizations would be around 20 per cent (including the cost of the owners' money). Investing this in a business would only be justified provided the business can earn at least this percentage.

Taking into account that all assets do not perform and that even the performing assets perform for only about two-thirds of the year, the targeted annualized rate of return jumps up to perhaps closer to 50 per cent.

(Please note this percentage return is with reference to return on investment [RoI] and not the margin of profit on sales.)

Never forget that you do not own a single asset that does not have a corresponding liability. You do not have a single liability that does not have a cost. And if your liabilities are effectively costing you perhaps 50 per cent, then it should hit you where it hurts if you discover a single asset that does not earn 50 per cent.

Once you understand this you will perhaps understand one of the biggest secrets of improving profitability.

6. Lazy assets are the most expensive

Assets take holidays; liabilities don't.

No banker says, 'Oh, you don't work on a Sunday, so you need not pay me interest for that day.'

Convert your non-performing assets to performing ones. Else get rid of them and release the money. The biggest non-performing asset is money lying in the bank.

In my opinion, a characteristic of successful businesses is shortage of money.

7. Never use short-term funds for long-term purposes

The liabilities' side of a Balance Sheet represents sources of money and the assets' side reveals uses.

All sources can be broadly categorized as either short-term sources (to be returned within one year) or long-term sources.

Similarly, uses can be classified as short-term (which will get liquidated within one year) and long-term.

Short-term assets also represent the gross working capital of an organization.

Working capital can be depicted like a cycle. It is also called the cash-to-cash cycle. After the completion of each cycle, cash comes back in the form of cash.

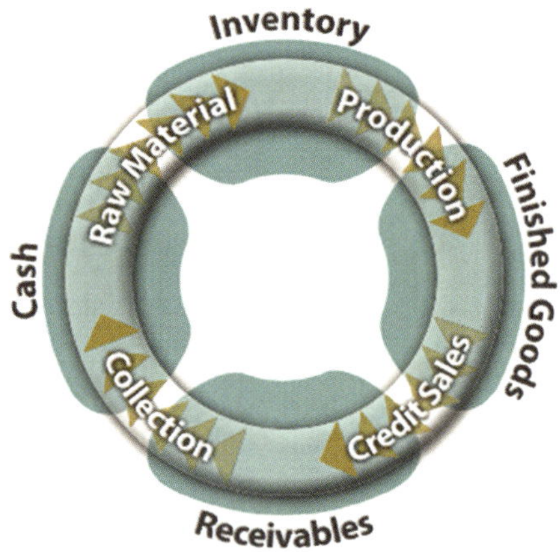

Short-term sources or liabilities are those which have to be paid back in a short period of time, maximum within one year. When it is time to pay these liabilities, it is essential that organizations have sufficient short-term assets which can be used to pay off the liabilities.

When short-term assets fall short of the short-term liabilities, organizations are forced to sell long-term assets to pay the short-term liabilities. This can severely jeopardize the health of a business.

To ensure that this eventuality does not arise, healthy organizations make it a point to ensure that the short-term assets (current assets) are always in excess of the short-term sources (current liabilities). In fact, it is desirable to maintain a current ratio (the ratio of currents assets to current liabilities) of 2:1.

Since all current assets cannot be liquidated at will (for instance, the inventory), the ratio of liquid assets to current liabilities, called the liquid ratio or the quick ratio, should be maintained at a minimum of 1:1.

Healthy organizations must ensure that long-term funds are used for long-term purposes and short-term funds for short-term purposes.

There is no harm if long-term funds are used for short-term purposes, but never ever use short-term funds for long-term purposes.

If there were a graveyard of failed companies, the tombstones in front of many would read: 'Here lies a company that used short-term funds to acquire long-term assets.'

This message should be engraved on stone and displayed prominently by entrepreneurs, so as to be constantly reminded: 'I will never, I repeat, NEVER, use short-term funds to acquire long-term assets.'

8. The concept of contribution

Profit is arrived at by deducting expenses from income.

However, all expenses can be broken up broadly into two types – variable and fixed.

Profit now becomes a function of sales (or income) less variable and fixed costs.

If you deduct variable costs from sales, the resultant figure is called contribution. And contribution less fixed costs gives profit.

Sales

(-) Variable Costs

= Contribution

(-) Fixed Costs

Profit

Once you understand this you will begin to get an insight into your numbers. It will help you take pricing decisions, the extent to which discounts can be offered and the maximum period of credit that can be extended to your customers. It will also help you work out the break-even point of your business. You will be able to understand the profit made merely by looking at the sales turnover achieved and will be able to work out the sales required to earn a desired amount of profit.

The key learning from the concept of contribution is that, if need be, you may sell at a loss, but, notwithstanding how compelling the circumstances may be, never sell at a negative contribution.

If profit is negative and contribution is positive you may eventually make a profit as volumes increase. But if you are generating a negative contribution, the more you sell the bigger the loss will be.

9. Higher the fixed costs, higher the profit

Leverage denotes a disproportionate impact on the bottom line due to a certain change in the top line.

Leverage is caused by the presence of fixed costs in an organization's costing structure.

To enjoy the benefit of leverage, it is essential to have fixed costs. Higher the fixed costs, greater the leverage benefit.

However, one must not invite fixed costs, as that will actually result in an increase in the total cost and a consequent reduction in profit.

What one can do instead is to swap a variable cost with a fixed cost where possible.

The advantage of higher fixed costs is that when sales increase only the variable costs increase proportionately; the fixed costs don't. This causes the overall costs to increase less than proportionately and the profit to go up exponentially.

The disadvantage of having fixed costs is that when revenues decrease, the costs don't decrease, leading to an equally disproportionate fall in profit.

When sales are in the ascendant, wherever possible, exchange variable costs with fixed costs, and when recessionary conditions set in, do the reverse – exchange fixed costs with variable ones. It will serve you well.

Part II MAKING FINANCIAL STATEMENTS

CHAPTER 2 How to Make a Balance Sheet the Layman's Way

A common misconception is that in order to learn how to read Balance Sheets, one must also know how to make them. This is not true at all.

It is quite possible to learn to read, interpret and understand Balance Sheets without knowing how they are made.

While everyone who is expected to read a Balance Sheet* need not know how to prepare one, it's really not as difficult as many fear it might be.

In fact, let me teach you how to make a Profit & Loss Account and a Balance Sheet in a jiffy.

But first, let us answer a few questions:

Where does all the data that goes into the Profit & Loss Account and the Balance Sheet come from?

It is, of course, contained in the accounting records of the organization.

How would you define accounts?

Accounts are a record of all financial transactions that take place in the organization during a particular period.

Why do organizations maintain accounts?

As we already know, the primary reason to start any business enterprise is to make profit. And profit, as seen earlier, is not so obvious. Therefore, all transactions that take place get recorded, and whatever gets recorded periodically gets compressed.

A compressed version of accounts is presented in the form of two financial statements. One is called a **Profit & Loss Account** and the other a **Balance Sheet**.

* *(I have used the words 'Balance Sheet' here to mean both Profit & Loss Account and Balance Sheet.)*

Now, this is important for you to understand, so I'm going to repeat it: All financial transactions get recorded as part of accounts. And when accounts are summarized, the result is presented in the form of a Profit & Loss Account and a Balance Sheet.

This means that everything that happens in an organization over a certain period must eventually appear either on the face of the Profit & Loss Account or the Balance Sheet.

The Profit & Loss Account and the Balance Sheet together reveal four types of transactions: expenses, incomes, assets and liabilities.

This, therefore, tells you that nothing can happen in an organization which is not eventually going to be categorized as one of these four.

There are only four possibilities for any transaction that takes place in an organization.

So, if you wish to make these financial statements the non-accountant's way, all you have to do is look at every transaction that takes place, examine it, assess whether it is an expense, an income, an asset or a liability, and record it accordingly. Your Profit & Loss Account and Balance Sheet will now be ready.

Imagine for a moment that your organization takes a decision to stop maintaining accounts. Instead, it keeps a large box in the middle of the entrance lobby and each time a financial transaction takes place, instead of recording it in the books, someone writes it on a piece of paper and drops it into the box.

At the end of a certain period this box is given to you and you are asked to make a Profit & Loss Account and a Balance Sheet.

Can you do it?

Of course you can.

How will you go about it?

First of all, keep a template of a Profit & Loss Account and a Balance Sheet in front of you, as shown here.

Profit & Loss Account

Expenses	Incomes

Balance Sheet

Liabilities	Assets

Now, put your hand in the box, take out the piece of paper one at a time, look at the item listed and try and identify whether it is an income, an expense, an asset or a liability, and record it accordingly.

Let's say, on the first piece of paper, 'salaries and wages' is written.

Where will you record it? This appears to be an expense.

The next piece says 'travelling costs'. Also an expense.

Goods or services sold? This is an income.

Loan taken? That's a liability.

Equipment purchased? An asset.

Interest paid on the loan? An expense, of course.

Rent and electricity payments? These are expenses.

Money invested in stocks of other companies? Assets.

Dividends received on these stocks? Income.

We can go on and on in this manner, and you will see that for every financial transaction you come up with (or every piece of paper that you take out of the box), you will be able to classify it as either an income, an expense, an asset or a liability.

At the end of the process you will find that the Balance Sheet you have prepared using our layperson's method is identical to the Balance Sheet prepared by your accountant.

Do you know your debits from your credits?

Debit and credit are two commonly used, yet greatly misunderstood, accounting words. I have rarely come across anybody who can confidently attribute a meaning to each of them. There is invariably a feeling that one is a gain, the other a loss; one is positive and the other negative – but it's hard to find any group of people who can reach a consensus on which is which.

The reason for this confusion is the fact that these two words, by themselves, have no meaning at all. They are used, primarily, in the context of the system of accounting in use almost all over the world, called the double-entry system of bookkeeping.

What is this system of bookkeeping?

The double-entry system works on the premise that each financial transaction that takes place will have an impact on two account heads simultaneously and the effect on each of the two account heads will be equal and opposite.

The words 'debit' and 'credit' are used to denote the two opposite effects of one transaction on two account heads.

One account must be debited and the other credited.

By themselves, these words represent neither good–bad, nor positive–negative. They simply represent two opposite impacts of one transaction on two account heads.

You now get further insight into Profit & Loss Accounts and Balance Sheets.

You know that every transaction that takes place has to be, by nature, either expense or income or liability or asset.

You have now learnt that for every transaction that takes place, the accountant will assign an account head, and label it either as **debit** or **credit**.

This means that of the four options (expense, income, liability or asset), two must be debits and two credits.

Take a look at this Profit & Loss Account and Balance Sheet, presented in the conventional T-format:

Dr **Profit & Loss Account** Cr

Expenses	Incomes
Raw Material	Sales
Salaries	
Stationery	
Interest	

Cr	Balance Sheet	Dr

Liabilities	Assets
Capital	**Fixed Assets** Land, Building, Machinery, Furniture
Reserves	
Long-Term Loans	
Current Liabilities Creditors, Bank Overdraft	**Current Assets** Bank Balance, Receivables, Inventory

You will notice that expenses and assets are both debits (Dr), while incomes and liabilities both have a credit (Cr) label.

What further insight does this give you?

This tells you that if both expenses and assets are labelled as debits, they must be similar in some way. On the other hand, incomes and liabilities must also have a similarity, since both carry the tag of credit.

Now, carefully examine the items appearing on the expenses' side and on the assets' side.

Do you see any similarity between expenses and assets?

Look at any expense, say **salary**; pick out any asset, say **furniture**.

Do you see any similarity between them?

The similarity between the two is that in both cases money goes out.

Both involve spending.

How are incomes similar to liabilities?

If both expenses and assets involve money going out, then incomes and liabilities must be bringing money in.

If I give you an amount of money, and in exchange purchase the goods that you are selling, this receipt of money will be income to you.

If I give you some more money, but this time as a loan, it will appear as a liability on your Balance Sheet.

A little while ago, I told you that it is so simple to make a Balance Sheet that all you have to understand is that there are only four options for any transaction that takes place in an organization: expense, income, liability and asset.

I'm now telling you that it is not just that simple. It is twice as simple!

Broadly speaking, all financial transactions can be divided into those that bring money in and those that take money out.

If money has come in, you now no longer have to choose out of four options to record it – you only have to choose between two: income or liability. If money goes out, choose between only two options – expense or asset.

Making a Balance Sheet the layman's way

Let us now learn how to make a Profit & Loss Account and a Balance Sheet directly from the details of the transactions, without going through the accountant's long and tedious method of accounting.

The purpose of this session is not to learn the formal way of making a Balance Sheet, but to take a common-sense, logical approach.

Illustration

Bobby starts a new furniture manufacturing business and calls it Globe Furniture.

What is the first step in starting a business? It is money. A business needs money to be set up.

Where will the money come from?

The first person it will approach is the owner.

You must remember that accounts are written in the books of the business (in this case, Globe Furniture). The owner will be considered an outsider. If Globe Furniture was set up as a corporate entity, it would actually be treated as a 'person' and the owner and the organization would be separate entities. But even if Globe was a proprietary concern of Bobby's, for accounting purposes, we will treat Globe as a separate entity and Bobby as a separate individual.

So when Globe needs money, it will first approach Bobby.

Let's imagine the total requirement of Globe is 250,000, of which Bobby agrees to contribute 100,000. This will be called Bobby's capital.

For the remaining 150,000, Globe approaches a bank for a loan.

It then invests 175,000 in infrastructure (land, building, machinery) to make furniture.

Having acquired infrastructure, it will need raw material. It purchases 60,000 worth of raw material on cash payment.

Globe also purchases raw material worth 25,000 on credit from a vendor called Rita, whom it promises to pay within a couple of months.

Now that it owns infrastructure and has also acquired raw material, it will hire people, spend money on overheads and all kinds of other manufacturing expenses. Let's say this amounts to 5,000.

By now its products are ready. It sells goods worth 75,000 on cash.

It also sells furniture worth another 50,000 to a customer called Neil on credit, the money to be received at a later date.

It has taken a loan from the bank. The bank demands interest at the rate of 10 per cent amounting to 15,000.

Globe has purchased raw materials from Rita and has not paid her. It now pays Rita 23,500.

And Neil, who has been sold goods on credit, pays Globe 40,000.

Globe Furniture	
Capital	100,000
Loan	150,000
Land, Building, Machinery	175,000
Raw Material (Cash)	60,000
Raw Material (on Credit for Rita)	25,000
Manufacturing Expenses	5,000
Sales (Cash)	75,000
Sales (on Credit to Neil)	50,000
Interest on Loan	15,000
Paid to Rita	23,500
Received from Neil	40,000

Let us now make a Profit & Loss Account and a Balance Sheet for Globe Furniture from a layperson's perspective, that is, without any knowledge of accounting, except what I have explained to you so far.

How should we go about it?

Step 1: Keep two blank formats in front of you, one titled Profit & Loss Account and the other Balance Sheet, as shown below:

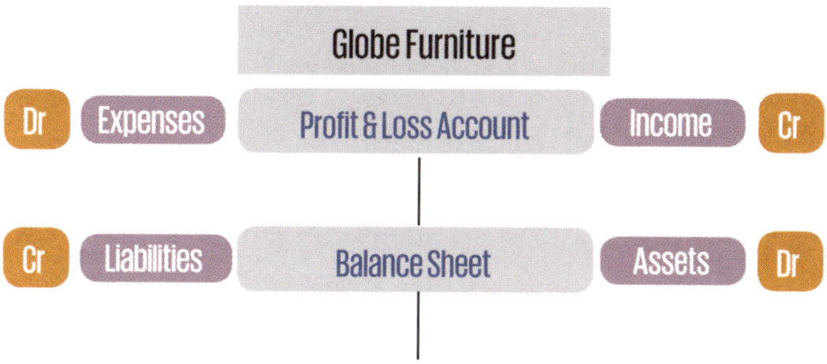

Step 2: Look at the transactions given above. Imagine this is the box that I was speaking about in the previous chapter. Every transaction that has taken place in the organization is written on a piece of paper and dropped into a box. You put your hand in the box and the first piece that comes out says, 'Bobby has introduced capital of 100,000,' on the second piece of paper is written, 'Loan taken 150,000,' and so on.

Step 3: Now look at each item and try and decide, there and then, whether it has resulted in an expense, an income, a liability or an asset, and record it accordingly on the appropriate side.

Either do this, or first look at the item and determine whether it has brought money in or taken money out, in which case you no longer need to choose out of four, but only out of two: if money has gone out, it will be either an expense or an asset, and if money has come in, you will have to choose between income and liability.

Let's try this method with a few transactions. The first item is capital. Has it brought money in or taken it out? This seems to be an inflow. Therefore, it can be either an income or a liability. This is definitely not an income, since it has not been earned.
So it must be a liability.

The second item is loan. This has also brought money in and seems to be a liability.

What about land, building, machinery purchased? This involves an outflow of money and you have to choose between an expense and an asset. These appear to be assets.

But hold on a minute…

You remember that I spoke about the double-entry system of book keeping earlier, while discussing debits and credits. As per the double-entry system, you have to record one transaction two times, because each transaction always has an impact on two account heads simultaneously.

If, as discussed above, you record capital as a liability, loan also as a liability, land and building as asset, you are only making a single entry.

So, in order to satisfy the double-entry system, you will have to examine each transaction, identify the two account heads that are affected and record each transaction two times.

When will the double-entry system be satisfied?

The double-entry system will be satisfied when each transaction gets recorded two times, and one effect appears on the debit side and the other on the credit side.

For instance, if 100 is recorded on the expenses' side (that is, on the debit side) the requirement of the double-entry system would have been complied with if another 100 is recorded on the credit side.

What are the options for this to happen?

The second 100 can either appear on the income or on the liabilities' side.

Is there a third option?

Actually, there is. It can also appear on the assets' side. But then it should be recorded as a (–) 100.

A negative figure on the debit side is tantamount to a credit and a negative figure on the credit side is equivalent to a debit.

In other words, a debit can appear either as a positive figure on the debit side or as a negative figure on the credit side. And a positive figure on the credit side or a negative figure on the debit side both amount to a credit effect.

Different options to satisfy the principles of double-entry bookkeeping

Option 1

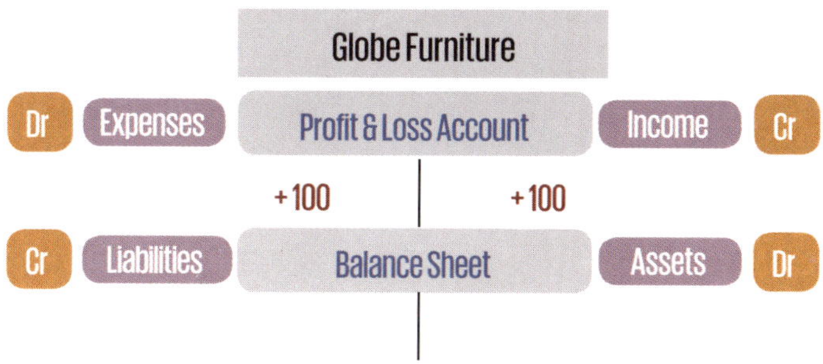

Option 2

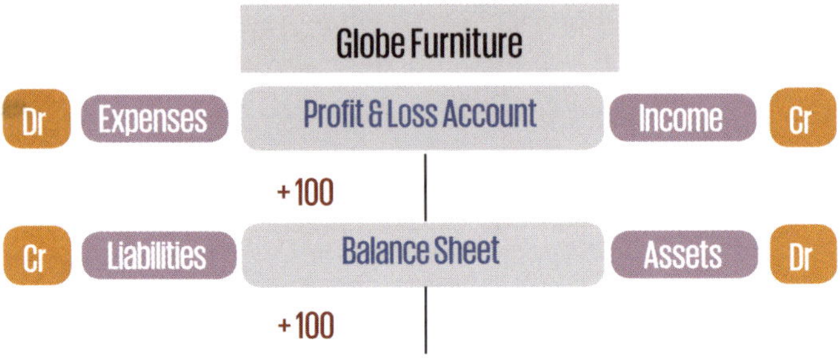

Option 3

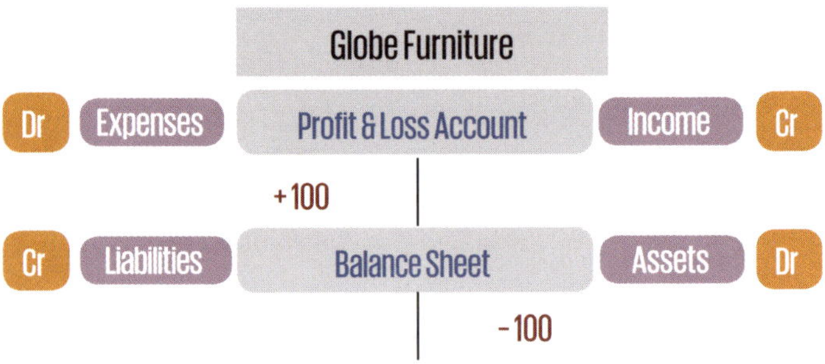

Option 4

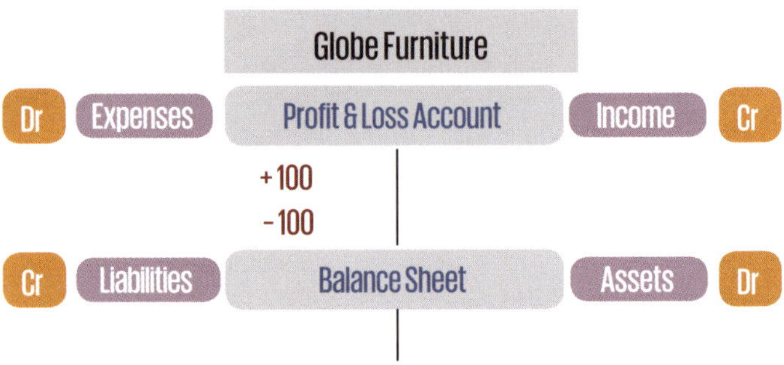

In fact, you don't need to worry about this. Debit and credit will happen on their own. You need to simply apply sound logic, identify the two dimensions of each transaction – the two account heads that are affected – and record it. If your logic is sound, you will find that one figure will automatically appear on the debit side and the other on the credit side.

If you find that you have recorded a transaction twice on the debit side or twice on the credit side, you simply need to re-examine the logic you have applied.

Let us see how this works.

Let us make a Profit & Loss Account and a Balance Sheet from the above data.

1. The first item is capital

Bobby has introduced a capital of 100,000 in the business.

As discussed above, this has brought money in and we need to choose between the account heads of income and liability when recording this in the Balance Sheet.

As already discussed, this appears to be a **liability** (credit effect).

What about the second effect?

In what form did Bobby bring this capital? In cash.

And where is this cash today? Globe Furniture is now in possession of cash of 100,000.

This is an **asset** for Globe (debit effect).

Please note, we didn't think at all about debit and credit. But because the logic applied was correct, automatically we have recorded once each on the debit and credit side.

Dr	Expenses	Profit & Loss Account	Income	Cr
Cr	Liabilities	Balance Sheet	Assets	Dr
	Capital	100,000	Cash 100,000	

2. The second item is loan

Globe Furniture has taken a loan of 150,000.

Again, money has come in and this seems to be a **liability** (credit effect).

And the second effect is that the cash in possession of the business has increased to 250,000 on the **assets'** side (debit effect).

Dr	Expenses	Profit & Loss Account	Income	Cr
Cr	Liabilities	Balance Sheet	Assets	Dr
	Capital	100,000	Cash ~~100,000~~ 250,000	
	Loan	150,000		

3. Land, building, machinery purchased for 175,000

Since this has taken money away, the choice is between assets and expenses.

These look like **assets**.

What about the second effect?

If you have, instinctively, said 'expense', stop for a minute.

If we record this item once as an asset and again as an expense, we would have recorded it twice on the debit side.

I told you a while ago, in such situations re-examine the logic.

Where are we going wrong?

We have discussed that money spent is either an expense or an asset, not both.

Since we are showing land, building, machinery (LBM) as assets, we cannot record them on the expenses, side again.

The second effect is that out of a cash balance of 250,000, Globe Furniture has spent 175,000 and the cash left with them is 75,000, as shown on the **assets'** side.

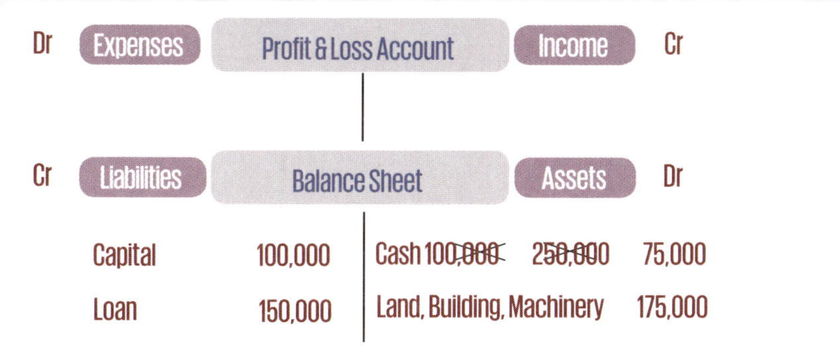

Let us double-check how debit and credit have been recorded?

When we put land, building, machinery on the assets' side, we gave it a **debit** effect. And the credit was recorded by deducting the same amount from cash on the assets' side. A negative on the debit side amounts to **credit**, remember?

But have you noticed that we are not consciously doing it? Debit and credit are happening on their own.

4. Raw material of 60,000 purchased on payment of cash

Money has gone out. Raw material seems be an expense (debit).

The second effect will be a further reduction of cash balance to 15,000 (credit).

Dr Expenses		Profit & Loss Account	Income Cr
RM	60,000		

Cr Liabilities		Balance Sheet	Assets Dr
Capital	100,000	Cash ~~100,000~~ ~~250,000~~ ~~75,000~~ 15,000	
Loan	150,000	Land, Building, Machinery	175,000

5. Raw material of 25,000 purchased on credit from Rita

Dr	Expenses	Profit & Loss Account	Income	Cr
	RM	~~60,000~~ 85,000		

Cr	Liabilities	Balance Sheet	Assets	Dr
	Capital	100,000	Cash ~~100,000~~ ~~250,000~~ ~~75,000~~	15,000
	Loan	150,000	Land, Building, Machinery	175,000
	Rita	25,000		

Purchase of raw material is an expense, as in the case of the previous transaction (debit). The total raw material purchased has now increased to 85,000.

The difference is that in this case, money has not been paid so far, and material has been purchased on credit from Rita.

Globe Furniture now owes 25,000 to Rita, who will appear as a creditor on the liabilities' side (credit).

6. Manufacturing expenses paid – 5,000

This is an expense (debit).

The second effect will be a reduction of cash on the assets' side to 10,000 (credit).

Dr Expenses	Profit & Loss Account	Income Cr
RM ~~60,000~~ 85,000		
Mfg Exp 5,000		

Cr Liabilities	Balance Sheet	Assets Dr
Capital 100,000		Cash ~~100,000~~ ~~250,000~~ ~~75,000~~ ~~15,000~~ 10,000
Loan 150,000		Land, Building, Machinery 175,000
Rita 25,000		

7. Goods sold (in cash) – 75,000

Sales is income (credit effect).

And it results in an increase in the cash balance on the assets' side to 85,000 (debit effect).

Dr	Expenses	Profit & Loss Account	Income	Cr

RM	~~60,000~~ 85,000	Sales	75,000	
Mfg Exp	5,000			

Cr	Liabilities	Balance Sheet	Assets	Dr

Capital	100,000	Cash ~~100,000~~ ~~250,000~~ ~~75,000~~ ~~15,000~~ ~~10,000~~ 85,000		
Loan	150,000	Land, Building, Machinery	175,000	
Rita	25,000			

8. Goods sold on credit to Neil – 50,000

Sales is still an income (credit). The only difference, in this case, is that money has not yet been received from Neil. The total sales have increased to 125,000.

Neil owes 50,000 to Globe Furniture, and will appear as a debtor on the assets' side (debit).

Dr	Expenses	Profit & Loss Account	Income	Cr

RM	~~60,000~~ 85,000	Sales	~~75,000~~ 125,000	
Mfg Exp	5,000			

Cr	Liabilities	Balance Sheet	Assets	Dr

Capital	100,000	Cash ~~100,000~~ ~~250,000~~ ~~75,000~~ ~~15,000~~ ~~10,000~~ 85,000		
Loan	150,000	Land, Building, Machinery	175,000	
Rita	25,000	Neil	50,000	

9. Interest paid to the bank at the rate of 10 per cent – 15,000

Interest paid is an expense (debit).

It also results in a reduction of cash on the assets' side, from 85,000 to 70,000 (credit).

Dr Expenses		Profit & Loss Account	Income Cr	
RM	~~60,000~~	85,000	Sales ~~75,000~~	125,000
Mfg Exp		5,000		
Interest		15,000		

Cr Liabilities		Balance Sheet	Assets Dr	
Capital		100,000	Cash ~~100,000~~ ~~250,000~~ ~~75,000~~ ~~15,000~~ ~~10,000~~ ~~85,000~~ 70,000	
Loan		150,000	Land, Building, Machinery	175,000
Rita	25,000		Neil	50,000

10. Amount paid to Rita against goods purchased on credit – 23,500

Rita is appearing as a creditor on the liabilities' side to the extent of 25,000.

Now that 23,500 is paid, Globe Furniture owes Rita merely 1,500. So this payment will reduce the figure of creditor appearing as a **liability** (debit).

And on the **assets'** side it will also reduce the cash balance by 23,500 and bring it down to 46,500 (credit).

Dr	Expenses		Profit & Loss Account	Income		Cr
RM	~~60,000~~	85,000	Sales	~~75,000~~	125,000	
Mfg Exp		5,000				
Interest		15,000				

Cr	Liabilities		Balance Sheet	Assets		Dr
Capital		100,000	Cash ~~100,000~~ ~~250,000~~ ~~75,000~~ ~~15,000~~ ~~10,000~~ ~~85,000~~ ~~70,000~~ 46,500			
Loan		150,000	Land, Building, Machinery		175,000	
Rita	~~25,000~~	1,500	Neil		50,000	

11. Amount received from Neil against goods sold on credit – 40,000

Similar to the previous transaction, Neil appears as a debtor on the assets' side. Since 40,000 is received from him, Neil is now a debtor merely to the extent of 10,000.

So, we should **reduce** the figure of the amount outstanding appearing against Neil's name by 40,000 on the **assets'** side (credit).

It will increase the cash balance on the same side by 40,000 (debit), taking it to 86,500.

Dr Expenses		Profit & Loss Account	Income		Cr
RM	~~60,000~~	85,000	Sales	~~75,000~~	125,000
Mfg Exp		5,000			
Interest		15,000			

Cr Liabilities		Balance Sheet	Assets		Dr
Capital		100,000	Cash ~~100,000~~ ~~250,000~~ ~~75,000~~ ~~15,000~~ ~~10,000~~ ~~85,000~~ ~~70,000~~ ~~46,500~~		86,500
Loan		150,000	Land, Building, Machinery		175,000
Rita	~~25,000~~	1,500	Neil	~~50,000~~	10,000

Now, let us find out if Globe Furniture has made a profit or a loss.

The total of the income is 125,000 and the total of the expenses is 105,000. Globe Furniture has made a profit of 20,000.

The convention is to write the heavier figure on both the sides, since all financial statements need to be balanced. And the balancing figure is shown on the side which has a lesser total.

So when an organization makes a profit, the figure must necessarily appear on the expenses' side, since the total of expenses is lesser than the total of incomes. (Conversely, if it makes a loss, the figure is shown on the income side.)

This profit needs to be transferred to the Balance Sheet.

Where will profit be shown? On the assets' or the liabilities' side?

Dr	Expenses		Profit & Loss Account	Income	Cr
RM	~~60,000~~	85,000	Sales	~~75,000~~	125,000
Mfg Exp		5,000			
Interest		15,000			
Profit		20,000			
		125,000			125,000

Cr	Liabilities		Balance Sheet	Assets	Dr
Capital		100,000	Cash ~~100,000~~ ~~250,000~~ ~~75,000~~ ~~15,000~~ ~~10,000~~ ~~85,000~~ ~~70,000~~ ~~46,500~~		86,500
Loan		150,000	Land, Building, Machinery		175,000
Rita	~~25,000~~	1,500	Neil	~~50,000~~	10,000

Profit will be shown as a liability.

Why should profit appear as a liability? Non-accounting persons will usually say that profit should be an asset.

Well, I will give you two answers for why profit appears as a liability, one a technical and the other a common-sense answer.

Technically speaking, is profit a debit or a credit balance?

Non-accountants will sometimes instinctively say that profits represent a debit balance, since they observe that it is written on the debit side of the Profit & Loss Account.

But a closer inspection will reveal that profit is a credit balance. The credit side of the Profit & Loss Account has a bigger total than the debit side. Profit, therefore, is a net credit. And it must accordingly appear on the credit side on a Balance Sheet, which is the liabilities' side.

The common-sense approach is that a business is started in order to make profit for the owners. The profit that a business makes belongs to the owners. And if the business has generated profit, and not yet distributed it amongst the owners, it is a liability for the business, since it owes this profit to them.

Profit will be shown in a Balance Sheet under a description called 'reserves', appearing immediately after capital.

(Just to set the record straight, in a proprietary concern or a partnership firm's Balance Sheet, profit is usually added to capital. In a limited company's Balance Sheet, it appears as reserves and surplus.)

So let us transfer the profit of 20,000 as reserves on the liabilities' side and see if the Balance Sheet balances.

Profit & Loss Account

Dr Expenses			Income		Cr
RM	~~60,000~~	85,000	Sales	~~75,000~~	125,000
Mfg Exp		5,000			
Interest		15,000			
Profit		20,000			
		125,000			125,000

Balance Sheet

Cr Liabilities			Assets		Dr
Capital		100,000	Cash ~~100,000~~ ~~250,000~~ ~~75,000~~ ~~15,000~~ ~~10,000~~ ~~85,000~~ ~~70,000~~ ~~46,500~~		86,500
Reserves (Profit)		20,000	Land, Building, Machinery		175,000
Loan		150,000	Neil	~~50,000~~	10,000
Rita	~~25,000~~	1,500			
		271,500			271,500

Voila! The Balance Sheet has balanced.

And we have made it simple by applying the short-cut formula that I explained in this chapter.

At the end of the book, I have given you one more case. It can be used by those of you interested in getting more familiar with making a Balance Sheet and a Profit & Loss Account using this method. The solution has also been provided for you to check the accuracy of your work.

Part III EVALUATING PROPOSALS AND FINANCIAL PERFORMANCE

CHAPTER 3 How to Evaluate Capital Expenditure Proposals

Let us now turn our attention to a very important topic, which is the evaluation of capital expenditure proposals.

What is a capital expenditure?

Capital expenditure (or CAPEX) can be juxtaposed with operating expenditure (or OPEX).

Consider an example of an operating expenditure decision.

Let's imagine you are on the lookout for a sales head for your company and are interviewing candidates for the position. You come across a very impressive candidate, with the right credentials and qualifications, who promises to do wonders to your top line. The candidate is very impressive but also very expensive. You are suitably impressed and decide to hire the person.

A month passes, two months pass, three months pass, and the person has generated no results. This candidate appears to have been very good at talking but not much else.

You realize your mistake and the person is given marching orders.

The mistake has been expensive. It has hurt you. But it will not cripple you. Why? Because, in this case, you have made an operating expenditure blunder.

But a mistake in evaluating a capital expenditure proposal can be critical and can sometimes even be the last mistake of one's life. This is because the amounts involved are much larger and the stakes far higher.

So, extra thought must necessarily go into the evaluation of CAPEX proposals.

Various techniques are used for evaluating capital expenditure proposals.

The age-old techniques used for this purpose are:

1. The **payback period technique**
2. The **average rate of return technique**
3. The third, and perhaps the most important and popular method being used globally today, is the **net present value technique**.

Let us discuss each of these methods in greater detail.

1. The payback period

Payback is the period within which the total cash inflows from the project equal the outflows involved in the project.

Since the key ingredient needed to work out the payback period is the cash flow, the most important step is to arrive at the cash flows from the project.

In order to arrive at the cash flow, non-cash expenses such as depreciation need to be ignored. However, depreciation is a tax-deductible expense and if it is ignored while arriving at taxable profit, you will end up arriving at a higher amount of profit before tax (PBT), and consequently a higher amount of tax payable.

What you need to do is to initially subtract the depreciation to arrive at the profit before tax, then calculate the tax payable at the appropriate rate and deduct it to arrive at the profit after tax. And to this, add back the depreciation deducted earlier to arrive at the cash flow.

Let us understand this with the help of an illustration.

Suppose a project costs 800,000 and the annual profit after depreciation at the rate of 12.5 per cent but before a tax of 50 per cent is 120,000.

The first step is to calculate the cash inflow.

Cash inflow from the project is:

Profit before tax	120,000
Less tax @ 50%	60,000
Profit after tax	60,000
Add back depreciation	100,000 (12.5% of 800,000)
Cash flow	160,000

Payback period = 800,000 / 160,000 = 5 years

2. The average rate of return

Accounting or average rate of return is the average annual yield of a project.

Under this method, the profit after depreciation and tax as percentage of total investment is considered. (Please note, in this method we don't need to arrive at the cash flow, so there is no need to add back the depreciation.)

Consider this illustration:

A project requiring an investment of 1,000,000 yields profit after tax and depreciation as follows:

Year	Profit after Tax and Depreciation
1	50,000
2	80,000
3	120,000
4	130,000
5	80,000
Total	460,000

After five years, the plant can be sold for 80,000.

Since the original investment in the plant was 1,000,000 and the salvage value at the end of the project is 80,000, the net investment in the project works out at 920,000.

The average rate of return can be calculated as follows:

$$\frac{\text{Total Profits} \times 100}{\text{Net Investment} \times \text{No. of Years}}$$

$$\frac{460{,}000 \times 100}{920{,}000 \times 5} = 10\%$$

3. The net present value

The net present value method is the best method for evaluation of investment proposals. It is also called the discounted cash flow technique.

This is the only method that takes into account the time value of money.

Let us first get clear about the terminology used while applying this method of evaluating capital expenditure proposals, particularly the following:

1. **Present value (PV)**
2. **Net present value (NPV)**
3. **Internal rate of return (IRR)**

1. Present value (PV)

What does present value or PV mean?

Imagine for a moment that I owe you a sum of money, say 100, today. And I give you a choice: you may take 100 today or you can take it from me next year.

Which option will you choose?

You will choose to be paid today.

Why?

Because you have avenues of investment available to you. If you take the 100 today and invest it in bonds that can earn for you 10 per cent per annum, by next year you would have made it into 110.

So, what is 110?

It is the future value of 100 today that can be invested at the rate of 10 per cent.

This future value concept we have all studied in school.

Let me repeat, 110 is the **future value of 100 today** invested at the rate of 10 per cent.

Now tell me, what is 100?

It is the **present value of 110 to be received next year**, which is discounted using a factor of 10 per cent.

What choice was offered to you? It was to take the 100 that I owe you today or to take it next year.

But 100 is the present value of 110 to be received next year. If I offer to give you 100 next year, in present-value terms I have paid you 91. You are a loser since I owe you 100 today.

Let's take another example.

This time I owe you 100 next year. And I give you a choice:

Take 100 next year or take 90 today.

Assuming you have the opportunity of investing the money and earning a return of 10 per cent, which option will you prefer?

You will prefer to take 100 next year.

Why?

Because the present value of 100 to be received next year discounted at the rate of 10 per cent is 91. (Which means 91 invested today at the rate of 10 percent will become 100 by next year. Whereas 90 will only become 99.)

Had I offered you 92 today, you should have accepted it.

But in case you had an opportunity to invest this money and earn a return of 12 per cent, even 90 would have been acceptable to you. This would be because the present value of 100 to be received next year, discounted at 12 per cent, is 89.

Businesses invest in a project today and generate revenues over a number of years in the future, and then compare the two to evaluate the project's viability. You are trying to compare two non-comparables. You cannot compare what is invested today with what will be earned in the future.

What you should do instead is to bring down the future cash flow to its present value and then a comparison can be made.

2. Net present value (NPV)

The net present value of a project is the sum of present values of all cash flows (inflows less outflows) associated with the project.

How to calculate the net present value

Let me list down the steps to arrive at the NPV of a project.

Step 1. Determine the cash outflow

Suppose a project requires an investment of 1,000,000.

Step 2. Determine the cash inflows

This can be done by adding depreciation to the profit after tax arising out of the project.

Suppose the project gives us cash inflows as shown below:

Year End		Cash Flows
1		115,000
2		114,000
3		139,000
4		141,500
5		136,500
6	Scrap Value	40,000
	Total	**686,000**

Step 3. Discount each inflow and work out its present value

For this purpose, the discounting rate must be determined.

Normally, the discounting rate equals the opportunity cost of capital.

Let us assume it is 10 per cent in this case.

To discount the cash inflows, we will also require a present value table for 10 per cent (see table below).

Year	Cash Inflows	Dis Factor @ 10%	Present Value
1	115,000	0.909	104,535
2	114,000	0.826	94,164
3	139,000	0.751	104,389
4	141,500	0.683	96,645
5	136,500	0.621	84,766
6	40,000	0.564	22,560
	686,000		507,059

Step 4. Arrive at the net present value

NPV = Discounted Value of Inflows (-) Discounted Value of Outflows

Discounted Value of Inflows	507,059
Less Discounted Value of Outflow	-500,000
= Net Present Value	= 7,059

The net present value of this project is 7,059.

What does it mean? Is it good enough? Should this project be taken up or not?

How much is the earning from this project? Is it 7.059?

That is not the correct answer.

Remember, we have already discounted the inflows?

At what rate was the discounting done? We used a discounting factor of 10 per cent.

This rate can either be called the hurdle rate, or the rate the promoters had decided should be the minimum return to be received in order to go ahead with this project.

What is left after discounting the inflows at 10 per cent is 7,059. This means that the earnings from this project are 7,059, over and above the 10 per cent.

If the criteria for acceptance was a minimum return of 10 per cent, this project can be accepted.

What if the promoters wanted a minimum return of 12 per cent in order to go ahead?

Then we would have to discount the inflows using a factor of 12 per cent.

Let's try doing that.

Now we have a negative NPV of 19809.

What does that mean?

It means the promoters wanted a minimum return of 12 per cent in order to accept this investment proposal, but the project is generating 19,809 lesser than 12 per cent.

If cash flow were discounted using the 12% factor

Year	Cash Inflows	Dis Factor @12%	Present Value
1	115,000	0.893	102,695
2	114,000	0.797	90,858
3	139,000	0.712	98,968
4	141,500	0.636	89,994
5	136,500	0.567	77,396
6	40,000	0.507	20,280
	686,000		480,191
	Less Outflow		500,000
	NPV		(19,809)

If the criteria for acceptance was a minimum return of 12 per cent, this project should be rejected.

3. Internal rate of return (IRR)

When we discounted the inflows using a factor of 10 per cent, we arrived at a positive NPV, indicating that the actual return generated by the project was higher than 10 per cent.

When we had applied a discounting rate of 12 per cent, we got a negative NPV.

Does it now give you an idea of the internal rate of return generated by this project, that is, the return that the project is actually earning?

It appears to be somewhere between 10 and 12 per cent.

So long as the NPV is positive, it indicates that the IRR is higher than the discounting rate used. If the NPV is negative, it indicates that the IRR is lower than the discounting rate. The rate at which the NPV is zero is the IRR of the project.

Rules for acceptance of a capital expenditure proposal:

The proposal can be accepted if NPV is positive.

It should be rejected if NPV is negative.

And if NPV is zero, it implies that the project generates cash flows at a rate equal to the rate of discounting used.

Let's understand this with the help of an illustration.

A company is contemplating purchasing a new machine. Two options, **EXX** and **WHY,** are available to choose from, each costing 400,000.

The expected cash flow generation from the two machines is as follows:

Year	Machine EXX CF	Machine WHY CF
1	40,000	120,000
2	120,000	160,000
3	160,000	200,000
4	240,000	120,000
5	160,000	80,000

Assuming this company's opportunity cost of capital is 10 per cent, let us compare the profitability of the two machines and decide which machine would be financially preferable.

First, add up the total cash flows in both the cases and check which machine generates a higher amount.

Year	Machine EXX CF	Machine WHY CF
1	40,000	120,000
2	120,000	160,000
3	160,000	200,000
4	240,000	120,000
5	160,000	80,000
	720,000	680,000

The total cash flow over the next five years expected from EXX is 720,000 and from WHY is 680,000.

Even though the investment in both the machines is the same, the total cash inflow from the first machine is higher than the other. Based on this assessment, EXX appears to be preferable.

This is the conclusion we will reach if we don't apply the NPV method of evaluation.

Let's try discounting the cash flows and work out the present value of the cash flows.

Year	DF@10%	Machine EXX		Machine WHY	
		CF	DCF	CF	DCF
1	0.91	40,000	36,400	120,000	109,200
2	0.83	120,000	99,600	160,000	132,800
3	0.75	160,000	120,000	200,000	150,000
4	0.68	240,000	163,200	120,000	81,600
5	0.62	160,000	99,200	80,000	49,600
		720,000	518,400	680,000	523,200
(-) Outflow			400,000		400,000
= NPV			118,400		123,200

There is now a paradigm shift in your perception of the profitability of the two machines. Even though the total cash inflow in EXX's case is higher than it is for WHY, in present value terms WHY is better than EXX. The NPV for EXX is 118,400, whereas it is 123,200 for WHY.

As I had mentioned earlier, this is the only method that takes into account the time value of money. It gives weight to the fact that it is not merely important to generate higher cash flows, but those ventures that bring higher cash flows earlier on in the life of the project and smaller cash flows later are better than those that bring smaller cash flows earlier and bigger ones later.

What if EXX was the only machine available?

If there was no choice and Machine EXX was the only option available, should this company go ahead and purchase this machine?

The answer in that case would be yes, they can go ahead.

Our criteria for selecting an investment proposal was that the NPV should be positive.

In the case of Machine EXX, the discounted value of the inflows is 518,400 while the outflows are 400,000, leaving behind a positive NPV of 118,400.

What does this tell us?

Since the opportunity cost for this company was considered to be 10 per cent, a positive NPV was indicative of the fact that an investment in this machine generated a return greater than 10 per cent.

But we also want to know how much the actual return is.

Let's try discounting the inflows using a higher percentage, say 15 per cent.

We are still getting a positive NPV. The machine is generating a return even higher than 15 per cent.

Machine EXX

Year	CF	DF@10%	DCF	DF@15%	DCF
1	40,000	0.91	36,400	0.87	34,800
2	120,000	0.83	99,600	0.76	91,200
3	160,000	0.75	120,000	0.66	105,600
4	240,000	0.68	163,200	0.57	136,800
5	160,000	0.62	99,200	0.50	80,000
	720,000		518,400		448,400
(-) Outflow			400,000		400,000
= NPV			118,400		48,400

So let's try using 20 per cent.

Machine EXX

Year	CF	DF @10%	DCF	DF @15%	DCF	DF @20%	DCF
1	40,000	0.91	36,400	0.87	34,800	0.83	33,200
2	120,000	0.83	99,600	0.76	91,200	0.69	82,800
3	160,000	0.75	120,000	0.66	105,600	0.58	92,800
4	240,000	0.68	163,200	0.57	136,800	0.48	115,200
5	160,000	0.62	99,200	0.50	80,000	0.40	64,000
	720,000		518,400		448,400		388,000
(-) Outflow			400,000		400,000		400,000
=NPV			118,400		48,400		(12,000)

Using a discounting rate of 20 per cent, we get a negative NPV.

The earnings from this machine are higher than 15 per cent, but lower than 20 per cent.

Are you now beginning to get an idea of the internal rate of return of this machine?

It appears to be somewhere between 15 and 20 per cent.

How to calculate the internal rate of return?

One method of working out the IRR, you would have gathered by now, would be to slowly increase the discounting rate, moving from 15 per cent and inching gradually towards 20 per cent. Somewhere along the way you will get a percentage at which the present values of inflows will match the discounted value of the outflow. That percentage will be the IRR.

But that would be too laborious a way of doing so.

Let me give you a simple formula to calculate the IRR.

In order to apply the formula, you will need a rate of discounting used at which the NPV is positive and another rate at which it is negative. We will call the former 'start rate' and the latter 'end rate.'

At the start rate, we get a positive NPV. We will call that 'surplus'. And at the end rate we arrive at a negative NPV. Let's call that 'deficit.'

To arrive at the IRR, you can apply the following formula:

Internal Rate of Return

$$= \text{Start Rate} + \frac{\text{Surplus}}{\text{Surplus} + \text{Deficit}} \times \begin{array}{l}\text{Difference between}\\ \text{Start Rate \& End Rate}\end{array}$$

(Please note, in the denominator in the formula we have **Surplus + Deficit**. Even though deficit is a negative number, it must be added to the surplus.)

Let us consider our start rate to be 15 per cent and the end rate to be 20 per cent and substitute the numbers in the formula.

$$= 15 + \frac{48{,}400}{48{,}400 + 12{,}000} \times 5 = 19\%$$

The internal rate of return for this machine is 19 per cent.

Part III EVALUATING PROPOSALS AND FINANCIAL PERFORMANCE

CHAPTER 4 How to Evaluate Financial Statements Using Ratio Analysis

Let me begin by asking you the most elementary question.

How to do ratio analysis?

To be effective, you should always do both an inter-company as well as intra-company comparison of ratios. In the case of the former, you must compare the organization with others from the same industry and figure out its standing vis-à-vis its peers. You should also perform intra-company analyses to understand whether, year after year, the organization is performing better or worse.

Which ratios can be calculated?

Types of Ratios

A. Profitability

B. Financial / Stability

C. Turnover / Velocity/ Activity / Efficiency

This will depend on the objective of doing the analysis.

Sometimes the objective is to understand how profitable an organization is. Then the ratios to be worked out will be called the profitability ratios.

Other times one may wish to understand how stable an organization is. The ratios to be calculated in such cases will be financial ratios or stability ratios.

Still other times the intention may be to know how efficient an organization is. The ratios that indicate efficiency go by different names like turnover ratios, velocity ratios, activity ratios or efficiency ratios.

Let us now study the three types and understand how to calculate and interpret each ratio.

A. Profitability

As the name suggests, the data to calculate these ratios will come from the Profit & Loss Account.

Take a look at this Profit & Loss Account.

Profit & Loss A/c			
Cost of Sales	90	Sales	120
Gross Profit	30		
	120		120
Operating Expenses	32	Gross Profit	30
Non-operating Expenses	2	Non-operating Income	10
Net Profit	6		
	40		40

Let us now see which ratios can be calculated using this Profit & Loss Account and what each ratio can tell us about its profitability.

1. The gross profit ratio

The first ratio that we can find out is the gross profit ratio.

For this we can use the following formula:

$$\text{Gross Profit Ratio} = \frac{\text{Gross Profit}}{\text{Sales}} \times 100$$

$$= \frac{30}{120} \times 100 = 25\%$$

This company has earned a gross profit of 30 on a sales turnover of 120, giving us a gross profit ratio of 25 per cent.

What is your reaction? Is this ratio impressive or not?

The answer is that, by itself, it means nothing. Ratio analysis should always be done either as an inter- or intra-company comparison.

Inter-company analysis:

If all the other companies in the same industry have a gross profit ratio in excess of 30 per cent, it is a definite sign of worry. And if the others are all lower than 20 per cent, one can justifiably be impressed.

Intra-company analysis:

One should check whether, year-on-year, this ratio is getting better or worse.

Let's say in Year 1 this company had sales of 120 and a gross profit of 30 and in Year 2 its sales have increased to 240. What should happen to the gross profit? Should the gross profit also increase to 60, or should it be lesser or greater than 60?

	Year 1	Year 2
Sales	120	240
GP	30	?
		60 <60 >60

Those of you who have read *Romancing the Balance Sheet* and recall the chapter on leverage analysis, which explains how there is an exponential impact on profit due to a certain increase in sales, may be thinking that in this case the gross profit should be greater than 60.

Let me remind you that leverage is caused by the presence of fixed costs in the costing structure.

Gross profit is arrived at by deducting the cost of sales from sales.

By nature, most of the components of cost of sales are variable and not fixed. Consequently, when sales increase by a certain percentage, the cost of sales also goes up by a similar percentage and so does the gross profit. Leverage effect has not set in yet.

So if sales of 120 becomes 240, chances are the gross profit of 30 will increase to 60.

But you discover that the gross profit has not increased proportionately to 60. It has either become less or more than 60.

What if it has increased less than proportionately to 58?

Sales has doubled, but gross profit has marginally less than doubled.

What is your reaction? Is there a reason to get worried?

If you are the owner of this business, I think you should lose your sleep.

Why?

The sales have doubled and the gross profit has almost doubled. Why should one get so concerned?

The answer is if there has been a one hundred per cent increase in sales and a less than one hundred per cent increase in gross profit, it means there must have been a more than one hundred per cent increase in cost of sales.

How can this happen?

It appears that the input costs must have gone up. The raw material suppliers and other vendors must have increased their prices.

When this company received a memo from its suppliers announcing a hike in prices, the company should have sent a similar memo to its customers announcing an increase in its selling prices too.

It appears that when its vendors increased their prices, it had no choice but to accept the hike, but when this company tried increasing the selling price of its products the customers were not willing to accept it.

The second way this could have happened is since the customers have purchased twice the quantity as before, they would have demanded and received better prices. But this company could not obtain a similar reduction in prices despite having also purchased twice the quantity of material as before.

It is a definite sign of weakness.

What if, on the other hand, the gross profit has increased to 62

In this case, the sales have doubled and the gross profit has more than doubled.

Now what is your reaction? Is there a reason to be happy?

Absolutely. It's celebration time. The reverse is happening.

The company appears to have hiked it selling prices and the customers accepted it. But when vendors tried increasing the input costs, this company did not need to accept the hike, maybe having other options available to it.

Or it could have happened that because its turnover has doubled, its purchases must also have doubled, and it was able to enjoy economies of scale obtaining quantity discounts from its vendors. But despite having sold twice the quantity, it did not have to offer similar discounts to its customers.

It is a sign of strength.

2. The net profit ratio

The net profit ratio can be calculated as:

$$\text{Net Profit Ratio} = \frac{\text{Net Profit}}{\text{Sales}} \times 100$$

The net profit is 6 on sales of 120, giving a net profit ratio of 5 per cent.

$$= \frac{6}{120} \times 100 \quad = 5\%$$

Say in Year 1 the company had sales of 120 and a net profit of 6. In Year 2, sales have doubled to 240. What should happen to the net profit? Can it more than double?

Now, the leverage principle will apply since certain fixed costs have also been deducted while arriving at the net profit.

What if you discover that the net profit has increased to 18? What is your reaction?

	Year 1	Year 2
Sales	120	240
NP	6	18

Is there a reason to be happy?

You do not even have a reason to smile.

Why? Sales have doubled and the net profit has trebled.

Shouldn't this be a cause for celebration?

The profit has increased disproportionately because when sales increased, certain costs which were variable in nature must have increased proportionately, but those costs that were fixed did not, such as the rent and salaries paid to certain staff, resulting in a less than proportionate increase in costs, and consequently a more than proportionate increase in net profit. There is no need to take credit for efficiency.

In fact, if one understood how to work out the leverage multiple (explained in *Romancing the Balance Sheet*) and knew that the multiple applicable to this company was, say 3, one would have known that if sales has doubled, the net profit should have increased by a factor of 3. The earlier profit was 6. Three times of 6 is 18. So, the profit in Year 2 should have been 24. Maybe somebody needs to be hauled up. Why has it increased to 18 and not 24?

It is so important to know what to be impressed by and what not to be impressed by. A marginal increase in the gross profit ratio is a tremendous achievement. A substantial jump in the net profit ratio may be nothing to write home about.

But the fact remains that if the sales of this company have gone up, its gross profit should have gone up at least proportionately and the net profit ratio should go up at a pace faster than the increase in sales.

3. Any expense or group of expenses to sales ratio

Virtually, any ratio can be calculated and it will give an insight into what is going on.

For instance, calculate the wages to sales ratio.

$$= \frac{\text{Wages}}{\text{Sales}} \times 100$$

If you find that the wage bill, compared to the previous year, has increased by 75 to 80 per cent and the production and sales has increased by maybe 15 or 20 per cent, it may appear that the workers' union is exceptionally strong.

On the flip side, if there has been a 20 to 25 per cent increase in wages and the production and sales has almost doubled, the workers appear to be earning every penny that is being paid to them.

Or, you may consider the advertising expenses to sales ratio.

$$= \frac{\text{Advertising Expenses}}{\text{Sales}} \times 100$$

If the advertising expenses have gone up significantly, say by 75 per cent or so, and the sales turnover has increased merely by 15 to 20 per cent, I think it is time to change the ad agency.

If, however, the advertising expenses have increased by about 20 per cent and the sales turnover has jumped up by maybe 70 to 75 per cent, you should hang on to the advertising agency that you are using. They seem to be doing a tremendous job.

Every ratio will provide an insight into what is happening in the company.

4. Operating ratio and the operating profit ratio

I have repeatedly emphasized on the importance of the bottom line; one should always remember business is not about generating sales but it is about generating positive and healthy profit.

No doubt, the bottom line is very important.

But there is something even more important than the bottom line.

Let's call it the semi-bottom line.

To explain what I mean, take a look at the Profit & Loss Account that we had made earlier once again.

Let's say that the numbers on that Profit & Loss Account pertain to Company A.

Let me now give you the numbers for Company B alongside.

Company B also has sales of 120, cost of sales of 90 and a gross profit of 30.

In addition, it has a non-operating income of 4.

On the expenses side, its operating expenses are 28 and the non-operating expenses are 9.

This company generates a net loss of 3.

Profit & Loss A/c

	B	A		B	A
Cost of Sales	90	90	Sales	120	120
Gross Profit	30	30			
		120			120
Operating Expenses	28	32	Gross Profit	30	30
Non-operating Expenses	9	2	Non-operating Income	4	10
Net Profit		6	Net Loss	3	
	37	40		37	40

Company A makes a profit of 6, while Company B makes a loss of 3.

What will you say if I ask you which is a better company? Which company are you more impressed by? Chances are your answer will be Company A – the one that makes a profit is obviously the better one.

This is the answer expected from you if you look at the bottom line.

But not if you look at the semi-bottom line.

To understand this, let's re-present the information from the Profit & Loss Account in a vertical form.

Sales less cost of sales will give gross profit, which is 30 in the case of both companies.

Gross profit is the income generated through the core activities of a business. It is the income earned through its regular operations.

If the company is a manufacturer of motor cars, then the income earned through making and selling cars is its operating income.

In addition, businesses may have non-operating incomes too.

		A		B
	Sales	120		120
(-)	Cost of Sales	(-) 90		(-) 90
	Gross Profit	30		30
(-)	Operating Expenses	(-) 32		(-) 28
	Operating Loss	(2)	Operating Profit	2
(+)	Non-operating Income	(+) 10		(+) 4
(-)	Non-operating Expenses	(-) 2		(-) 9
	Net Profit	6	Net Loss	6

If the car manufacturing company sells some spare land that it owns and makes a profit on the deal, this would be a non-operating income.

Expenses can be similarly divided into those incurred to run the core operations and those that are non-operating in nature.

Operating incomes and expenses have a pattern; a certain predictability. Non-operating incomes and expenses are unpredictable in nature. These may be there in a certain year and may be missing the next.

When you deduct operating expenses from gross profit you arrive at operating profit (or loss).

Add the non-operating income and deduct the non-operating expenses to arrive at the net profit.

Company A has a gross profit of 30 and its operating expenses are 32. On operations it makes a loss of 2.

Its bottom line, however, is positive. It makes a net profit of 6. This is because it has a non-operating income of 10 and non-operating expenses of merely 2. These, as pointed out earlier, are unusual in nature. They may not recur.

Company A has a negative semi-bottom line and a positive bottom line.

Company B also earns a gross profit of 30. Its operating expenses are 28. This tells us that to earn 30 it needs to spend 28. It makes an operating profit of 2.

However, because it has a non-operating income of merely 4 and non-operating expenses of 9 (which may not be there in the following years), it suffers a net loss of 6.

Company B has a positive semi-bottom line and a negative bottom line.

I will definitely support Company B over A.

Profit is usually calculated at two stages – gross profit and net profit. I am urging you to get into the habit of calculating it at three stages – gross profit, operating profit and net profit. And having a positive operating profit and a negative net profit is better than having a negative operating profit and a positive net profit.

This gives us two more ratios.

1. Operating ratio: I want you to note that the name operating ratio is not given to the ratio of operating profit to sales, but to the ratio of operating expenses to sales.

$$\text{Operating Ratio} = \frac{\text{Operating Expenses}}{\text{Sales}} \times 100$$

2. Operating profit ratio: For the operating profit ratio, the name itself uses the words operating profit.

$$\text{Operating Profit Ratio} = \frac{\text{Operating Profit}}{\text{Sales}} \times 100$$

The second formula for calculating this ratio: **100 – Operating Ratio**.

This means if, for instance, the operating ratio is 86 per cent, the operating profit ratio will have to be 14 per cent.

5. Net profit to capital employed ratio

The net profit to capital employed ratio looks at the earnings as compared to the capital invested in the business.

Since capital employed includes borrowed capital, the profit to be considered should be before rewarding the owners as well as the lenders, that is, the profit before interest and tax (PBIT).

The formula to calculate the net profit to capital employed ratio would then be:

$$= \frac{\text{PBIT}}{\text{Average Capital Employed}} \times 100$$

A point to be noted here is the denominator has a prefix 'average' attached to it, whereas it does not appear in the numerator.

This is because the numerator comes from the Profit & Loss Account, whereas the denominator has been derived from the Balance Sheet.

The fundamental difference between these two statements is that the former is for a period and the latter is as on a particular date; a snapshot so to say.

If the figure of profit in the numerator is, let's say, an annualized number, then the denominator representing the capital employed should be annualized too. Averaging it is an attempt to do precisely that.

6. Interest Coverage Ratio

Who do you think would be interested in this ratio?

Yes, the bankers.

Before bankers lend, they need to ensure that the borrower will be in a position to service the loan. They would like to know how many times they are covered.

If a borrower approaches a bank requesting a loan, the interest obligation on the loan he is seeking will be 100 per annum. The borrower has projected a sales turnover of 2,000.

Do you think the banker is well covered so far as the interest payable by the borrower is concerned?

The banker doesn't really care about the sales turnover. The reason being the bank is not the first one to be paid out of the turnover of 2,000. There are expenses that take precedence over the bank.

Salaries payable to the staff, payments to vendors, rent to the landlord – all these and other operating expenses will be paid first.

	Sales	2,000
(-)	Operating Expenses	1,700
=	PBIT	300
(-)	Interest	100

The PBIT is 300 and the interest obligation is 100. The interest coverage ratio works out to three times.

Interest Coverage Ratio

$$= \frac{\text{PBIT}}{\text{Interest}} = \frac{300}{100} = 3 \text{ times}$$

7. Dividend coverage ratio

Who would be interested in this ratio? The shareholders.

Not all shareholders though, since not all are interested in making money through receiving dividends. There are shareholders whose interest purely lies in an appreciation of the capital market valuation of the shares. As a result, there are several companies that have not paid a penny as dividend for years together and yet witness a steady rise in the market price of the shares.

However, investors who purchase shares with the intention of making money through dividends would naturally like to know their chances of getting the desired dividends.

What should be the formula to calculate the dividend coverage ratio?

Dividends are paid out of profit after tax (PAT).

While working out the interest coverage ratio, we had compared the PBIT with the interest commitment.

What do we compare the PAT with? Interest is a commitment, whereas dividend is not. So, the person calculating this ratio must compare the PAT with the dividend expectation.

	Sales	2,000
(-)	Operating Expenses	1,700
=	PBIT	300
(-)	Interest	100
=	PBT	200
(-)	Income Tax (say)	60
=	PAT	140
(-)	Dividend Expectation	70

Let's say, in order to receive the dividend that the shareholder is hoping to receive, the company will have to distribute 70.

The PAT is 140, the expected dividends is 70. This shareholder is covered two times.

In case the PAT was 210, the dividend coverage would be three times.

If the PAT was 280, it would be four times.

What does a higher coverage ratio indicate?

The higher the ratio, the greater the probability that the shareholder will receive the expected dividend.

Dividend Coverage Ratio

$$= \frac{\text{Divisible Profit}}{\text{Expected Dividend}} = \frac{140}{70} = 2 \text{ times}$$

B. Financial/Stability Ratios

Now, let's check out a few ratios that indicate the stability of a business.

The data for these ratios will be taken from the Balance Sheet.

So, let me show you a Balance Sheet.

Balance Sheet

Share Capital	200		Fixed Assets		600
Reserves	100	300	Current Assets		400
Long-term Loans		600	Inventory	120	
			Debtors	200	
Current Liabilities		100	Bank Balance	80	
		1,000			1,000

1. Current ratio

This ratio is also called the working capital ratio or the solvency ratio or the 2:1 ratio.

The ratio compares the current assets with the current liabilities and can be worked out as:

$$= \frac{\text{Current Assets}}{\text{Current Liabilities}}$$

As per the Balance Sheet, the currents assets are 400 and the current liabilities are 100, giving us a current ratio of 4:1.

$$= \frac{400}{100} = 4:1$$

Current liabilities represent short-term liabilities – the liabilities which will mature over a short period of time, no later than one year. When it is time to pay off these liabilities, it is essential at that time to have a sufficient amount available in the form of current assets; those assets that can be liquidated within the next one year. The money released through the liquidation of current assets can be used to pay the current liabilities.

If current assets fall short of the current liabilities, then organizations are forced to sell their fixed assets to meet short-term liabilities. This is definitely not a sign of a stable organization.

The norm is that healthy organizations must try and maintain a current ratio of about 2:1.

(Readers of *Romancing the Balance Sheet* will recall the discussion we had on this ratio as part of the explanation of the second golden rule of good finance management.)

2. Liquidity ratio

This ratio is also called the quick ratio or the acid-test ratio or the 1:1 ratio.

When the current liabilities come knocking on the doors demanding payment, there should be sufficient current assets available to meet the short-term liabilities.

However, all current assets are not available to make payments.

Current assets broadly have three components:

1. Inventory
2. Debtors
3. Cash and bank balances

Of these three, the most liquid is the third one – the cash and bank balances.

Relatively less liquid are the debtors, which are not sitting in the bank in liquid form but are near-liquid by nature. If not immediately, these can be liquidated soon and then can be used to make payments.

The least liquid is inventory. There is no saying when a customer will be found and the inventory will be sold.

If the current liabilities are, say 10, even if the current assets are 30, it will be of no use if out of 30, inventory alone is 25.

Out of the three components of current assets, if we ignore inventory, the other two are then called liquid assets or quick assets. The ratio of liquid assets to current liabilities is called the liquidity ratio or the quick ratio.

$$= \frac{\text{Liquid Assets}}{\text{Current Liabilities}}$$

As per the Balance Sheet, out of total current assets of 400, if we eliminate inventory of 120, it will give us liquid assets of 280. And the current liabilities are 100. This gives us a liquidity ratio of 2.8:1.

$$= \frac{280}{100} = 2.8:1$$

The norm for a healthy liquid ratio is a minimum of 1:1.

3. Proprietary ratio

As per the Balance Sheet, the total assets are 1,000 and the proprietor's funds (that is, the owner's capital comprising share capital and reserves) are 300. This gives us a proprietary ratio of 0.3:1.

$$= \frac{\text{Proprietor's Funds}}{\text{Total Assets}}$$

$$= \frac{300}{1000} = 0.3:1$$

This indicates that of the total assets owned by this company, 30 per cent have been funded out of owners' money.

Who feels happy when this ratio is higher? It is the banker. Bankers love it when owners have more skin in the game.

4. Debt-equity ratio

This is the ratio between the long-term debt and the shareholders' funds.

Shareholders' equity includes equity and preference share capital.

It shows the relationship between borrowed funds and ownders' capital and is a popular measure of long-term financial solvency of an entity.

In this ratio, debt is always in the numerator.

$$= \frac{\text{Long-term Debts}}{\text{Equity}}$$

$$= \frac{600}{300} = 2{:}1$$

So a debt-equity ratio of 2:1 would indicate that debt is two times of equity.

A highly leveraged company enjoys the advantage of an exponential growth in profit due to the benefit of trading on equity, while at the same time making it riskier.

Looked at from the creditors' perspective, it represents a danger signal indicating that the owners are putting lesser money of their own.

From the owners' point of view, it indicates that with a limited investment of their own, they can retain control over the company as well as avail of high returns on their investments.

A low debt equity ratio has the opposite implications.

5. Repayment coverage ratio

While discussing profitability ratios, we had seen the interest coverage ratio.

Before agreeing to extend a loan, bankers would be interested in checking the borrower's ability to service the loan.

Similarly, bankers would also like to check the borrower's ability to repay the principal.

In the case of interest coverage ratio, we had compared the PBIT with the interest commitment.

What should be the numerator for the repayment coverage ratio?

To repay principal sums of the loan, what is required is cash flow or the availability of funds.

And what do we compare this with?

We will compare the available funds with the installments of long-term loans due within the year.

Repayment Coverage Ratio

$$= \frac{\text{Available Funds for Repayment of Long-Term Debts}}{\text{Long-term Loan Installments Due within a Year}}$$

C. Turnover/Velocity/ Efficiency/Activity Ratios

These ratios indicate how efficient an organization is. The norm is the higher the ratio, the greater the efficiency.

One should consciously try and increase each of these ratios.

The numerator for all these ratios will be the turnover. The question is what is meant by turnover? Usually, turnover refers to sales. But for the purpose of these ratios, you may use sales as turnover, or you may use cost of sales.

However, in case cost of sales is used, you must take care that it is done for all the ratios. And, in the case of inter-company analysis, you should ensure that cost of sales is considered in the numerator for the other company too.

For the purpose of illustrating these ratios, I will consider sales as turnover.

To calculate these ratios, let's consider the following Profit & Loss Account and Balance Sheet.

Profit & Loss A/c

CoS	900	Sales	1,200
GP	300		
	1,200		1,200
Op Exps	320	GP	300
NO Exp	20	NO Inc	100
NP	60		
	400		400

Balance Sheet

Sh Cap	200		FA		600
Res	100	300			
			CA		400
LTL		600	INV	120	
			Drs	200	
CL		100	Bank	80	
		1,000			1,000

Let us discuss a few turnover ratios now.

1. Net working capital turnover ratio

To calculate this ratio, we will use the following formula:

$$= \frac{\text{Turnover}}{\text{Average Working Capital Employed During the Year}}$$

You will notice that the word 'average' appears in the denominator when it is not used in the numerator.

We have discussed this earlier while considering the net profit to capital employed ratio.

I had pointed out that when one figure is taken from the Profit & Loss Account (which is for a period) and the other from the Balance Sheet (which is as at a certain date), the two numbers are non-comparable. If the Profit & Loss Account is for one year, then we will need to annualize the Balance Sheet figure too.

The turnover is 1,200 and the net working capital (current assets less current liabilities) is 300. (Let's assume this is also the average working capital.)

$$= \frac{1{,}200}{300} = 4 \text{ Times}$$

The net working capital turnover ratio works out to 4 times.

Remember, the higher the ratio, the greater the efficiency.

2. Inventory turnover ratio

The closing inventory appearing in the Balance Sheet is 120. Assuming this company's opening inventory was 80, this gives us an average inventory of 100. The turnover is 1,200. The inventory turnover ratio works out to 12.

$$= \frac{\text{Turnover}}{\text{Average Inventory Held During the Year}}$$

$$= \frac{1,200}{100} = 12 \text{ Times}$$

If another company from the same sector has an average inventory of 150 and a turnover of 1,500, its ratio would be 10 times. That company is less efficient.

The higher the ratio, the greater the efficiency.

3. Capital employed turnover ratio

With a capital employed of 900, this company has generated a sales turnover of 1,200.

$$= \frac{\text{Turnover}}{\text{Average Capital Employed During the Year}}$$

$$= \frac{1,200}{900} = 1.33 \text{ Times}$$

In the following year, if the turnover increases without an increase in the capital employed, it will indicate greater efficiency.

On the other hand, if the capital employed increases by 50 per cent and the turnover increases by 25 per cent, it will indicate reduced efficiency.

4. Fixed assets turnover ratio

This company has fixed assets of 600 and a turnover of 1,200, giving a fixed assets turnover ratio of 2:1.

$$= \frac{\text{Turnover}}{\text{Average Fixed Assets Used During the Year}}$$

(For this ratio, instead of sales, the value of production can be used in the numerator.)

$$= \frac{1200}{600} = 2\ \text{Times}$$

5. Debtors outstanding and debtors turnover ratio

Debtors Outstanding Ratio

$$= \frac{\text{Average Trade Receivables Outstanding}}{\text{Average Daily/Weekly/Monthly Credit Sales}}$$

The annual sales of this company are 1,200. That is, its average monthly sales are 100.

The amounts receivable represented by debtors are 200.

$$= \frac{200}{100} = 2\ \text{Months}$$

This indicates that two months' sales are outstanding. It also indicates that this company offers 60 days' credit, on an average, to its customers.

Debtors Turnover Ratio

$$= \frac{\text{Credit Sales}}{\text{Average Trade Receivables}}$$

$$\frac{1{,}200}{200} \quad 6 \text{ Times}$$

Since two months' sales are pending, it gives us a debtors turnover ratio of 6.

If the debtors outstanding ratio was one month, it would give a debtors turnover ratio of 12.

In case the debtors outstanding ratio was three months, the debtors turnover ratio would be 4.

Remember, the higher the turnover ratio, the greater the efficiency.

6. Creditors payment ratio

Just as debtors are linked to sales, creditors are linked to purchases.

The creditors payment ratio can be worked out using the following formula:

$$= \frac{\text{Average Trade Payables}}{\text{Average Daily/Weekly/Monthly Credit Purchases}}$$

You could be wondering what does average daily/weekly/monthly credit purchases, appearing in the denominator, mean.

Often debtors and creditors are expressed in terms of either the number of days, weeks or months.

For example, one may say that the credit period offered to debtors, or that offered by creditors, is two months. Or the credit period is eight weeks. Or it is sixty days.

If your creditors are 200,000 and the weekly purchases are 25,000, then the creditors are equal to eight weeks' purchases.

Part IV TRACING CASH AND FUNDS FLOW

CHAPTER 5 How to Make and Read a Cash Flow Statement

Readers of *Romancing the Balance Sheet* will recall the stress I had laid on making profit – that one should always remember business is not about generating top lines but about maintaining bottom lines.

I had also explained at great length that profit did not automatically translate into money. It is quite possible for a business to make a huge profit and yet have no cash, and vice versa.

Along with a focus on the bottom line, it is equally important for an organization to ensure that it has sufficient cash available at all times. There is no pleasure in making profit if at the end of the month the business does not possess the money to pay salaries.

Successful companies stand on two pillars:

1. The ability to generate profit
2. The ability to effectively manage cash flows

Both the pillars need to be strong for the sustained growth of a business. If one is and the other isn't, it is a matter of time before the business will get into trouble.

If your business is making a profit, you have won half the battle. The other half will depend upon how well you manage your cash flows.

If the cash flow management is deficient, the very fact that the company is making a profit could be the reason for its collapse.

How can that happen?

That can happen because profits raise expectations. When a company makes profit, the employees who have been largely responsible for its good performance expect to be rewarded by way of bonus. Similarly, the government of the country in which the business operates expects income tax. And the owners of the business, the shareholders, expect to be paid dividends.

The business will be forced to distribute the profit generated among these three interested parties. And most of these payments are non-negotiable. Letting down of any of them entails consequences.

Non-payment of bonus could lead to labour unrest and even strikes. Non-payment of income tax has serious legal repercussions. Letting down the shareholders could adversely affect the market price of the company's stock and hamper its future ability to raise funds.

So a company that makes profit often finds itself forced to distribute the entire profit. In the absence of requisite cash flow, the ramifications could be challenging.

Having emphasized the importance of these twin pillars of profit and cash flow, it must also be kept in mind that during times of recession the first pillar takes a back seat, and the second one, namely cash flow management, becomes more important.

During recessions, profitability of most businesses is hit, but which are the companies that cannot cope? It is those that run out of cash.

You must remember that recessions don't last forever. You need to outlast the recession. And businesses where cash runs dry are the ones that cannot.

On the flip side, companies that are sitting on a pile of cash during recessions are the ones that can make a killing. Because recessions also throw up opportunities. There are great companies that are up for grabs during downturns, available to be taken over at throwaway prices. But the opportunity is lost on many because there is no cash available.

Businesses that practice good finance management, those that are bottom-line driven and that ensure effective cash flow management at all times, perform better than others during boom times and, more importantly, are the ones that survive when the times are tough.

To monitor and to keep control on cash flows, one must regularly prepare and read the cash flow statement.

In this chapter let me dwell upon the cash flow statement.

What is included in a cash flow statement?

A cash flow statement divides the receipts and disbursements into three broad categories:

Inflows and outflows on account of

1. **Operating activities**
2. **Investing activities**
3. **Financing activities**

1. Operating activities are the regular business operations of the organization. Operating cash inflows would include receipts from sales of goods or services as also the revenues from interest and dividends. The operational expenditures are considered as outflows. A point to be noted here is that although interest expenses are included here, the dividends paid are not. Dividends are considered a part of financing activity.

2. Investing activities include the sale of property, plant and equipment or marketable securities as inflows, and purchasing of property, plant and equipment or marketable securities as cash outflows.

3. Financing activities include receipts from borrowing money or issuing stock as inflows. The outflows occur when loans are repaid or treasury stocks are purchased or dividends are paid to stockholders.

Cash flows are classified into:

Operational cash flows

Cash received or expended as a result of the company's internal business activities

Investment cash flows

Cash received from the sale of long-life assets, or spent on capital expenditure (investments, acquisitions and long-life assets)

Financing cash flows

Cash received from the issue of debt and equity, or paid out as dividends, share repurchases or debt repayment

Let us take a simple case and construct a cash flow statement from the summarized cash account shown below.

Summarized Cash Account

To Balance b/f	5,000	By Payment to Suppliers	200,000
To Equity Shares	30,000	By Purchase of Fixed Assets	20,000
To Amounts Received		By Overheads	20,000
from Customers	280,000	By Salaries	10,000
To Sale of Fixed Assets	10,000	By Taxation	25,000
		By Dividends	5,000
		By Repayment of Loan	30,000
		By Balance c/f	15,000
	325,000		325,000

A. Cash Flow from Operating Activities:

Received from Customers	280,000	
Paid to Suppliers	(200,000)	
Paid for Overheads	(20,000)	
Paid for Salaries	(10,000)	
Cash Generated from Operations	50,000	
Income Tax Paid	25,000	
Net Cash from Operating Activities		25,000

B. Cash Flow from Investing Activities:

Purchase of Fixed Assets	(20,000)	
Sale of Fixed Assets	10,000	
Net Cash Used in Investing Activities		(10,000)

C. Cash Flow from Financing Activities:

Issue of Equity Shares	30,000	
Repayment of Loans	(30,000)	
Payment of Dividends	(5,000)	
Net Cash Used in Financing Activities		(5,000)
Net Increase in Cash		10,000
Add Opening Cash		5,000
Closing Cash Balance		15,000

How is a cash flow statement different from a cash budget?

A cash flow statement is historical in nature. It shows the cash inflows and outflows which have already taken place in the past. On the other hand, a cash budget is futuristic. It shows cash inflows and outflows which are expected to take place in the future. In other words, **a cash budget is a projected cash flow statement.**

How does a cash flow statement help?

Since the cash flow statement reveals the liquidity position of the company, it shows if the company will be able to fund its operations from internal accruals or if it will need to seek outside funds. This helps businesses to prepare for lean periods and downturns.

It also shows the extent to which the company's operations have contributed to cash flow. It is not only important for a company to earn economic value for its shareholders – it must convert that to cash too.

It reveals the extent to which the company is investing in its own business by way of capital expenditure or expanding its business through strategic acquisitions and investments.

The cash flow statement also shows the extent to which the company has been successful in returning value to shareholders or whether it had to tap the capital markets in order to fund its operations and investing activities. Companies with high cash balances and low levels of debt are ideal for those looking for new investments. The statement of cash flows will highlight how successful a company has been in its efforts to generate cash and reduce debt.

A good company will seek to generate positive free cash flow. Free cash flow is the cash flow left after recovering not merely the operating expenditure but also the essential capital expenditure, for instance, on equipment and machinery, which is necessary to maintain its competitive edge.

The cash flow statement also throws light on the stage of a company in its life cycle, that is, whether it is a growing company, a mature one or in its decline.

A growing company may have a negative cash flow from operating and investing activities and a positive cash flow from financing activities as it continues to consume money to grow.

A mature firm will have a positive cash flow from operating activities and possibly a negative balance in its investing activities.

A declining firm may have a positive cash flow from operating and investing activities and a negative cash flow from financing activities as it uses money from its business to pay back its investors.

Part IV TRACING CASH AND FUNDS FLOW

CHAPTER 6 How to Make and Read a Funds Flow Statement

What is a funds flow statement?

As its name suggests, the two sides of a funds flow statement reveal the sources and uses of funds, that is, where the money has come from and where it has gone.

Sources	Funds Flow Statement	Uses

To prepare a funds flow statement we will need two Balance Sheets.

If you wish to prepare an annual funds flow statement, you will need the previous year's Balance Sheet as well the current one. If you wish to prepare a monthly funds flow statement, you will need two Balance Sheets one month apart, and so on.

Let's consider a quick illustration.

The Balance Sheet shown here reveals the previous year's figures on the left and the current year's figures on the right.

In order to prepare a funds flow statement you will need to examine every item on the liabilities' side and each item on the assets' side, and try to reach a conclusion whether there has been an inflow or an outflow of funds.

For instance, the first item on the liabilities' side is share capital. It was 100 in the previous year and the following year it has increased to 300.

Sources	Balance Sheet		Uses		
Previous Year		Current Year	Previous Year		Current Year
100	Share Capital	300	600	Fixed Assets	750
75	Reserves	200			
500	Long-term Loans	400	175	Current Assets	300
100	Current Liabilities	150			
775		1,050	775		1,050

What does it indicate? It appears that fresh capital of 200 was raised during the year and would accordingly be recorded on the sources' side of the funds flow statement.

The next item is reserves. There has been an increase of 125 (from 75 to 200). Now we know that the profit earned is transferred to reserves. And profit represents income earned. This will also be shown as a source.

The next item, long-term loans, shows a reduction from 500 to 400, which indicates a repayment of loan. So, 100 will appear on the uses' side of the funds flow statement.

On the assets' side, the first item is fixed assets, which shows an increase of 150, from 600 to 750. Apparently, this company has purchased fresh fixed assets during the year. This, therefore, will be shown on the uses' side.

Up to this stage, the funds flow statement is looking as shown here:

Sources	Funds Flow Statement		Uses
Issue of Shares	200	Loan Repaid	100
Profit	125	Purchase of FA	150

You will notice, so far I have done nothing with the current liabilities and the current assets. This is because you must not look at these two individually, but together as representing net working capital, which is the difference between current assets and current liabilities.

Typically, a funds flow statement will be accompanied by another statement showing change in working capital. And we will transfer the net decrease or increase in working capital as either a source or a use.

In the previous year, the current assets were 175 and the current liabilities 100, giving you a net working capital of 75. In the current year, the current assets are 300 and the current liabilities 150. The net working capital is 150.

Change in Working Capital Statement		
CA	175	300
- CL	100	150
= W Cap	75	150
Increase in W Cap	75	

There is an increase in the net working capital of 75 (150 less 75).

An increase in net working capital represents a use of funds. More money has been invested in working capital.

And now our funds flow statement is ready.

Sources		Uses	
Issue of Shares	200	Loan Repaid	100
Profit	125	Purchase of FA	150
		Increase in W Cap	75
	325		325

The Balance Sheets showed total liabilities of 775 in the previous year and 1,050 in the current year, but the funds flow statement reveals that the money flowing in and out of this business was to the tune of 325.

Let's assume the numbers are in millions. A cursory glance at this funds flow statement shows total receipts of 325 million.

Before one gets too happy, it will be necessary to understand that the entire receipt does not represent profit. Of this sum, the profit is merely 125 million. The balance of 200 million has come by way of a loan from the owners.

Nevertheless, the most important question is if 325 million has come in, where is it? It is certainly not visible on the bank statement.

The answer to this will be provided by the uses' side. Of the 325 million, this organization has used 100 million to return a loan. Another 150 million has been used to purchase some fixed assets and yet another 75 million has been invested in working capital. We could have dived in further and found out how much has been invested in each component of working capital.

It gives you a bird's-eye view of the total sources and uses of money. This helps in ascertaining whether the rules of good finance management have been followed or not, whether or not this organization has been using long-term funds for long-term purposes and the short-term funds for short-term purposes, and so on.

The key thing to remember here is that nothing must appear as a source unless it has actually brought money in. Nothing must be shown as a use unless money has actually been spent.

One needs to critically examine every item to ensure that what apparently appears to be a source has also brought in money.

For instance, when we looked at the first item, the increase in share capital, we concluded that because share capital has increased by 200 there must have been an inflow of that sum.

But is it possible that the share capital may have increased but money may not have come in? It is.

During the year gone by, this company could have declared a bonus issue of one free share for every two held.

The share capital of the previous year stood at 100. The bonus issue would have taken it up to 150. But this accretion to share capital did not bring any money in. The increase of capital from 150 to 300 must have been in cash.

So now, there is a change in the amount to be recorded on the sources' side. We realize that the inflow on account of issue of shares is 150, and not 200.

Sources	Funds Flow Statement		Uses	
Issue of Shares	~~200~~	150	Loan Repaid	100
Profit		125	Purchase of FA	150
			Increase in W Cap	75
		275		325

But now the funds flow statement does not balance. The total of the sources' side is 275, while that of the uses' side is 325. There has to be another effect of this new piece of information about the bonus issue of shares.

Bonus is essentially a conversion of reserves into shares. Originally the Balance Sheet revealed reserves at 75 in the previous year and at 200 in the current year.

Now that we know that a bonus issue of 50 has been made, it means that 50 has been transferred from reserves to share capital. So, reserves of 75 must have first reduced to 25 and then grown to 200 in the current year. This tells us that the profit for the year was 175 (200 less 25) and not 125 as originally presumed.

Sources		Funds Flow Statement		Uses
Issue of Shares		150	Loan Repaid	100
Profit	~~125~~	175	Purchase of FA	150
			Increase in W Cap	75
		325		325

Let's consider yet another scenario.

We know that the value of fixed assets increases with acquisitions and decreases due to depreciation.

In the Balance Sheet, the fixed assets stood at 600 in the previous year and at 750 in the current year. Looking at this we had assumed that the cost of fixed assets purchased during the year was 150.

But what if we are informed that depreciation of 75 had been provided on the fixed assets during the year. How does it change our perception?

We know now that there will be two repercussions of this.

1. The original assumption that fixed assets increased from 600 to 750 gets invalidated. This is because the current year's figure of 750 is after providing for a depreciation of 75. This means that fixed assets, which at the beginning of the year stood at 600, must have first increased to 825, and after deducting the depreciation we must have arrived at the closing value of 750.

So, the cost of assets purchased during the year is 825 less 600, that is, 225.

Incorporating this in the funds flow statement takes the total of the uses' side to 400.

Sources		Funds Flow Statement		Uses
Issue of Shares	150	Loan Repaid		100
Profit	175	Purchase of FA	~~150~~	225
		Increase in W Cap		75
	325			400

2. The second implication of this would be on the profit, which appears on the sources' side at 175. The profit is arrived at after deducting depreciation, which appears as an expense. However, depreciation is a non-cash expense, that is, it reduces the profit but does not take away any money. For the funds flow statement, as pointed out earlier, we are merely interested in the profit that came in the form of money and not the book profit.

Sources			Funds Flow Statement	Uses
Issue of Shares		150	Loan Repaid	100
Profit	~~175~~	250	Purchase of FA	225
			Increase in W Cap	75
		400		400

We now realize that the cash profit is more by 75 (adding back the depreciation to the book profit). So, the revised perception of profit that will appear as a source would be 250 (that is, adding back the depreciation of 75 to the profit of 175 as perceived earlier).

To sum up, in order to prepare a funds flow statement, we need to prepare three statements:

1. A funds flow statement.
2. A statement showing the change in working capital, where the current assets and current liabilities are recorded to determine whether there has been an increase or a decrease in working capital, and accordingly transfer it to the funds flow statement.
3. An adjusted profit statement, where the book profit is recorded initially, which gets adjusted due to the effect of non-cash items (if any) to arrive at the cash profit which will get transferred to the funds flow statement.

The rules of preparing a funds flow statement can be summarized as follows:

1. An increase in liability is a source. (In our example, share capital had increased. Our conclusion was that fresh capital has been raised.)
2. A decrease in liability is a use. (When we saw that the amount of loan had decreased, the conclusion was that it must have been repaid.)
3. An increase in assets is a use. (One assumes that an increase in fixed assets is due to fresh purchases having been made.)
4. Conversely, a decrease in fixed assets is a source.
5. An increase in working capital represents a use. (More money must have been invested in working capital.)
6. A decrease in working capital represents a source. (Money blocked in working capital must have been released.)

The thing to be kept in mind is that the initial impulse on applying the above rules must be validated. That is, we must confirm that what appears to be a source has actually brought in the money and what we think is a use has actually taken money away. Only then should it be recorded on the funds flow statement.

Rules

↑ in Liability = Source	↑ in Assets = Use	↑ in W Cap = Use
↓ in Liability = Use	↓ in Assets = Source	↓ in W Cap = Source

Let us now make a funds flow statement and then try and read it too.

Study the Balance Sheet shown below.

Balance Sheet

Equity Share Capital	1,000	Land & Building	500
Reserves & Surplus	178	Plant & Machinery	1,450
Term Loan	600	Investments	-
Debentures	500	Stocks	800
Bank Overdraft	50	Debtors	500
Creditors	1,020	Bank Balance	98
	3,348		3,348

What do you see?

The liabilities' side reveals this company has an equity capital of 1,000. The retained profit represented by reserves and surplus is 178. The term loan outstanding is of 600 and the amount borrowed through the issue of debentures is 500. It has a bank overdraft of 50 and it owes its creditors 1,020.

On the assets' side, we find it has fixed assets, between land, building and machinery of 1,950 and its current assets are worth 1,398 (made up of inventory of stocks worth 800, debtors and receivables of 500 and it has a bank balance of 98).

Can you read much from this? Not really.

Let's say the above Balance Sheet is for the second year.

Let me now give you the figures for the first year alongside.

Balance Sheet					
	Yr 1	Yr 2		Yr 1	Yr 2
Equity Share Capital	1,000	1,000	Land & Building	500	500
Reserves & Surplus	140	178	Plant & Machinery	900	1,450
Term Loan	600	600	Investments	200	-
Debentures	900	500	Stock	1,300	800
Bank Overdraft	-	50	Debtors	450	500
Creditors	840	1,020	Bank Balance	130	98
	3,480	3,348		3,480	3,348

The following additional information has been provided:

1. Depreciation of 150 was provided on plant and machinery for the year.
2. The debentures were redeemed at a premium of 3 per cent.
3. The company has distributed dividends of 375 among its shareholders.

You are also informed that the sales of this company, over the two years, have been more or less constant.

Does this information throw some more light on the financial position of this company?

To make more sense of these two Balance Sheets, and to get a better idea of the health of this company, let's make a funds flow statement using the two years' data given.

In order to prepare a funds flow statement, let us first keep the formats ready.

The first format required is of the funds flow statement itself.

Sources	Funds Flow Statement	Uses

The second will be for the statement showing change in working capital.

Change in Working Capital Statement		
Current Assets	Y1	Y2
Current Liabilities		

And the third format we will need to prepare is an adjusted profit statement, where the book profit will get transferred initially.

Adjusted Profit Statement
Profit

1. The first item on the Balance Sheet is equity capital. There has been no change. So there appears to be no fund flow on this account.
2. The second item is reserves. It has increased from 140 to 178, indicating that additional profit of 38 has been transferred to reserves during the year. Since this may or may not represent cash profit, it will initially be transferred to the adjusted profit statement.
3. The next item is the term loan. There is no change to this number too.
4. We now have debentures showing a decrease of 400, from 900 to 500.

Debentures represent borrowed money, and a reduction in the figure must be due to repayment of the loans, or on account of redemption of debentures. At first glance, it appears that this must have entailed an outflow of funds to the extent of 400. However, the additional information tells us that debentures were redeemed at a premium of 3 per cent. This means that even though debentures carrying a face value of 400 were redeemed, the cash flow that took place was 412 (that is, 400 plus premium at the rate of 3 per cent of 400, that is, 12). This will be shown on the uses' side.

However, you must remember that the reason a funds flow statement is always balanced (that is, the total of both the sources' and the uses' sides is the same) is because it is prepared from the difference between two Balance Sheets, which are also balanced. This tells you that the impact on the funds flow statement should be exactly the difference between two Balance Sheet figures.

So, when you see that debentures were 900 in the first year and 500 in the second year, the difference is 400. The impact on the funds flow statement should be to the extent of 400. However, when we record 412 on the uses' side, having realized that this is the cash outflow on account of debenture redemption, we have recorded a number which is greater than the difference between the two Balance Sheet figures. This tells us that there must be another implication of 12 yet to be recorded on the sources' sides in order to bring the net impact on the uses' side of the funds flow statement to 400.

Sources	Funds Flow Statement	Uses
	Debentures Redeemed	412

The second implication is when we understand that the premium of 12 paid during redemption must have been recorded as an expense on the Profit & Loss Account and the profit of 38, which has been transferred to the adjusted profit statement, is after deducting this amount. However, if we show this amount on the face of the funds flow statement as a use, as we have done, then we have recorded the same item twice. (Once when it was deducted as an expense while arriving at the profit and again when we record 412 instead of 400 on the funds flow statement).

So, we must add it back to the profit in the adjusted profit statement.

Adjusted Profit Statement	
Profit	38
Add Back:	
Premium on Redemption of Debentures	12

5. The next two items, bank overdraft and creditors, are current liabilities and can be directly transferred to the working capital statement.

Change in Working Capital Statement

Current Assets	Y1	Y2
Current Liabilities		
Bank O/d	-	50
Creditors	840	1,020

6. On the assets' side, the first item is land and building. There is no change, so we need not do anything.
7. Next is plant and machinery, which has increased from 900 to 1,450. This increase of 550 appears to be on account of acquisition of more machinery and should be transferred to the uses' side. However, we see from the additional information given that depreciation of 150 was provided during the year. This tells us that 1,450 of plant and machinery appearing at the end of Year 2 is after reducing the depreciation. This means the value of machinery before adjusting for depreciation must have been 1,600 (1,450 plus 150). We now realize that at the end of Year 1 the plant and machinery stood at 900 and at the end of Year 2 it was 1,600, so the cost of machinery purchased during the year is 700.

   Also, the depreciation of 150 has been shown as an expense in the Profit & Loss Account. Since it is a non-cash expense, it has reduced the profit but has not reduced the cash. So, for the purpose of preparing a funds flow statement, it should be added back to the book profit appearing in the adjusted profit statement in order to arrive at the cash profit.

Adjusted Profit Statement	
Profit	38
Add Back:	
Premium on Redemption of Debentures	12
Depreciation on Plant	150

Sources		Funds Flow Statement	Uses
		Purchase of Plant	700
		Debentures Redeemed	412

8. The next item is investments, which stood at 200 in Year 1 and has been reduced to nil in Year 2. In the absence of any contrary information, we can assume that these investments were disposed of. Since there is no information provided on whether the investments were sold at a profit or a loss, we will assume these were sold at par. Accordingly, 200 can be shown as a source.

Sources		Funds Flow Statement	Uses
		Purchase of Plant	700
Investments Sold	200	Debentures Redeemed	412

9. The following three items are current assets and can be transferred to the statement showing change in working capital.

Change in Working Capital Statement

	Y1	Y2
Current Assets		
Stock	1,300	800
Debtors	450	500
Bank Bal	130	98
Current Liabilities		
Bank O/d	-	50
Creditors	840	1,020

Let's take another look at the Balance Sheets and additional information provided at the beginning to check whether all the information has been taken into account or not.

Balance Sheet

	Yr 1	Yr 2		Yr 1	Yr 2
Equity Share Capital	1,000	1,000	Land & Building	500	500
Reserves & Surplus	140	178	Plant & Machinery	900	1,450
Term Loan	600	600	Investments	200	-
Debentures	900	500	Stock	1,300	800
Bank Overdraft	-	50	Debtors	450	500
Creditors	840	1,020	Bank Balance	130	98
	3,480	3,348		3,480	3,348

The following additional information has been provided:

1. Depreciation of 150 was provided on plant and machinery for the year.
2. Debentures were redeemed at a premium of 3 per cent.
3. Dividends of 375 were distributed among the company's shareholders.

You are also informed that the sales of this company, over the two years, have been more or less constant.

We have considered every item appearing on the Balance Sheet which has involved a flow of funds. However, we still have one piece of additional information provided to us that we have not yet accounted for. That the company had distributed a dividend of 375 among its shareholders.

The first impression is to do nothing, because a funds flow statement is prepared with the help of two Balance Sheets. This item does not appear on the Balance Sheet, but as a footnote.

When dividend was paid, it must have been transferred to the Profit & Loss Account as an expense and would have also reduced the company's bank balance.

But if we don't show this item on the face of the funds flow statement, the reader of this statement will have no way of knowing that the company has distributed the dividend.

In the interest of maximum disclosure, if we wish to show the dividend paid as an outflow on the uses' side, then it should be added back to the profit in the adjusted profit statement.

Sources		Funds Flow Statement	Uses
		Purchase of Plant	700
Investments Sold	200	Debentures Redeemed	412
		Dividend Paid	375

Adjusted Profit Statement	
Profit	38
Add Back:	
Premium on Redemption of Debentures	12
Depreciation on Plant	150
Dividend Paid	375

Now let us complete preparing the funds flow statement by first transferring the total of the adjusted profit of 575 on the sources' side.

Adjusted Profit Statement	
Profit	38
Add Back:	
Premium on Redemption of Debentures	12
Depreciation on Plant	150
Dividend Paid	375
	575

Now we can also find out the change in the working capital.

Current assets in the first year were 1,880 and the current liabilities were 840, giving us a net working capital of 1,040.

Similarly, the net working capital in the second year works out to 328. There has been a reduction in working capital of 712, which also represents a source. Money which was blocked in working capital has been released.

Change in Working Capital Statement			
Current Assets		Y1	Y2
Stock		1,300	800
Debtors		450	500
Bank Bal		130	98
Current Liabilities	A	1,880	1,398
Bank O/d		-	50
Creditors		840	1,020
	B	840	1,070
Working Capital	A-B	1,040	328
Decrease in Working Capital			712

We will accordingly show this 712 on the sources' side of the funds flow statement.

Sources	Funds Flow Statement		Uses
Profit	575	Purchase of Plant	700
Investments Sold	200	Debentures Redeemed	412
Decrease in Working Capital	712	Dividend Paid	375
	1,487		1,487

And now the funds flow statement is ready, showing a total inflow and outflow of 1,487.

Let us now try and read this funds flow statement.

Take a close look at this funds flow statement and the statement showing change in working capital that we have just prepared and see what it can tell us about the financial health of this organization.

(For the purpose of reading, I am assuming that the numbers in the statements we have prepared are in '000s.)

Funds Flow Statement

Sources		Uses	
Profit	575,000	Purchase of Plant	700,000
Investments Sold	200,000	Debentures Redeemed	412,000
Decrease in Working Capital	712,000	Dividend Paid	375,000
	1,487,000		1,487,000

Sales of the company have been constant over the last two years.

Change in Working Capital Statement

		Y1	Y2
Current Assets			
Stock		1,300,000	800,000
Debtors		450,000	500,000
Bank Bal		130,000	98,000
Current Liabilities	A	1,880,000	1,398,000
Bank O/d		-	50,000
Creditors		840,000	1,020,000
	B	840,000	1,070,000
Working Capital	A-B	1,040,000	328,000
Decrease in Working Capital			712,000

A look at the statement reveals a total inflow of 1.487 million. Of this, 575,000 has come from profits, 200,000 from the sale of certain investments and 712,000 has been released from working capital.

This money was used to purchase a new plant for 700,000, to redeem debentures worth 412,000 and to reward shareholders by paying dividends of 375,000.

Let's first analyze the sources.

At this stage, we cannot pass any comment on the volume of inflow, since numbers are relative in nature. We are not even aware of the sales turnover of this organization. Is it in hundreds of thousands or in tens of millions? If the former, then a 1.487 million funds flow would be huge, and it would be loose change if the latter was the case.

Since there is limited information available, I will confine my comments to where the data is provided and refrain from commenting where it is not.

A sum of 575,000 has come from profits. The footnote informs us that sales are constant over the two years. But it does not mention whether profit is constant or not.

With the same turnover as in the previous year, if the profit was less than last year, it is a sign of concern, and if it is more, it is a positive indicator.

However, the fact remains that this is a profit-making organization and that is always a good sign.

The company has disposed of some investments and generated an inflow of 200,000.

The use of the word 'investments' indicates that it must have been an investment made not for its core activities. This organization appears to have invested money outside its business in earlier years, but during the current year it felt the need to dispose of the investments and plough the money back into its own business.

To that extent, this also appears to be a positive sign.

The working capital has been reduced drastically (we know it's a drastic reduction since it is responsible for almost half the inflow). Despite this, sales have been constant. **To be able to maintain the top line with substantially reduced working capital at its disposal appears to indicate efficiency.**

The uses' side reveals that a plant has been purchased at a cost of 700,000, which forms a major part of the uses of funds.

Buying a plant, which results in the creation of more capacity, is indicative of plans for expansion and growth, which is definitely a positive sign.

This company has used 412,000 towards redemption of debentures at a premium of 4 per cent.

Honouring commitments and repaying debts, that too at a premium, gives this company a few more brownie points.

Finally, the organization has also distributed dividends of 375,000 among its shareholders.

The profit earned by the organization is 575,000 and dividends distributed are 375,000, which amounts to over 65 per cent of the profit.

If you were contemplating investing in this company, this could be one of its most attractive features.

A cursory look at this funds flow statement can leave one with the impression that this organization is in terrific shape.

But hold on a minute.

Did we apply a single rule that I have explained in this and the earlier book? Did we calculate any ratio? None at all.

What we have done just now is an emotional analysis of the statement.

Let's take another look at the funds flow statement, check the application of the rules of good financial management and reassess our comments on the health of this business.

The first area of concern in this statement is the footnote, which says that the sales over the last two years have been constant.

I would usually not recommend investing in an organization unless the sales graph is facing skywards. Why would I want to go out of my way and invest in a company whose sales have either started stagnating or falling? This footnote worries me.

However, let me not be hasty and write this company off merely on the basis of a footnote.

I have always felt that the function of a funds flow statement is less to supply answers and more to help you frame the right questions. One can then form opinions based on the information received.

Before I reach any conclusion, I would like to meet an important functionary of this organization, preferably the CEO, and ask a couple of questions.

The first question I have for the CEO is: Why have your sales stopped growing?

The second question: Even though your sales have not increased, why have you made this substantial investment in a plant?

What if the CEO smiles pleasantly and tells me that their sales not growing is nothing to worry about?

The sales have remained the same not because they did not have orders – they are, in fact, overloaded with orders – but because they ran out of capacity.

It's precisely for this reason that they have made an investment in a new plant.

An answer like this would obviously bring about a paradigm shift in my outlook. My concern about sales not increasing, as also about the investment in plant, has been alleviated.

But now I have another question for the CEO.

If the organization has plenty of orders on hand, and now the capacity has also been created, it would mean that the company expects to produce and sell more in the coming months.

It is also natural, therefore, that to support the increased levels of activity, the company will need larger amounts of working capital.

However, the funds flow statement shows a drastic reduction in working capital.

So, my next question to the CEO is: How do you explain this contradiction?

On one hand, you have purchased a plant, indicating increased levels of activity. On the other, we can see that a large portion of the money required to fund the purchase has come through a reduction of working capital!

I now begin to fear that even though this organization is flush with orders and has the requisite installed capacity to increase production, it will not be able to scale up. It seems to me very likely that it is going to run short of working capital.

Keeping this doubt at the back of our minds, let us first do a clinical analysis of this funds-flow statement and see if the company has complied with the fundamental rules of good financial management, which demand that healthy organizations:

- Must use long-term funds for long-term purposes.
- Must use short-term funds for short-term purposes.
- MAY use long-term funds for short-term purposes.
- Must NEVER use short-term funds for long-term purposes.

Sources		Funds Flow Statement			Uses
Profit	LTS	575,000	Purchase of Plant	LTU	700,000
Investments Sold	LTS	200,000	Debentures Redeemed	LTU	412,000
Decrease in W Capital	STS	712,000	Dividend Paid	LTU	375,000
		1,487,000			1,487,000

Let's evaluate how the organization fares on this front.

The profit of 575,000 is a long-term source.

So are the sale proceeds of investments of 200,000.

However, 712,000 from reduction of working capital is a short-term source.

This means that the total long-term sources amount to 775,000 and the short-term sources to 712,000.

On the uses' side, purchase of a plant – 700,000 – is a long-term use.

Redemption of debentures of 412,000 is also a long-term use.

So is the dividend distribution of 375,000.

Or, since dividend is necessarily a distribution of profits, a better way of looking at this would be to eliminate 375,000 from the uses' side as well as from the profits on the sources' side.

The new equation that emerges is:

Total long-term sources = 400,000 (profits after deducting dividends + sales proceeds of investments)

Short-term sources = 712,000 (reduction of working capital)

However, **the entire utilization of funds of 1,112,000 is on the long-term account!**

It is obvious that this organization has been guilty of using short-term funds for long-term purposes!

Let us now turn our attention to the **statement showing change in working capital** again and see if this organization can afford to reduce its working capital.

Change in Working Capital Statement

Current Assets		Y1	Y2
Stock		1,300,000	800,000
Debtors		450,000	500,000
Bank Bal		130,000	98,000
Current Liabilities	A	1,880,000	1,398,000
Bank O/d		-	50,000
Creditors		840,000	1,020,000
	B	840,000	1,070,000
Working Capital	A-B	1,040,000	328,000
Decrease in Working Capital			712,000

A healthy organization will ensure that it maintains a current ratio (current assets: current liabilities) in the region of 2:1 and a quick ratio (liquid assets: current liabilities) of a minimum of 1:1.

The current ratio in Year 1 works out to 2.24:1 (1880,000 / 840,000), which is higher than the norm of 2:1.

In Year 2, it has reduced drastically to 1.31:1 (1398,000 / 1070,000), which is way below the norm.

As I have explained earlier, current ratio falling below the norm may not, by itself, be a cause for concern as long as the quick ratio is maintained at 1:1 or more.

Let's now quickly calculate the quick ratio.

The quick ratio in Year 1 is 0.69:1 (580,000 / 840,000), well below optimum.

In Year 2, it has fallen further to 0.56:1 (598,000 / 1070,000), which is even lower.

This organization had a good current ratio in Year 1, which has become bad in Year 2.

It had a bad quick ratio in Year 1 itself, which has worsened in Year 2.

Does this appear to be an organization which can afford to reduce working capital?

Certainly not!

Now let's go into the details of the working-capital statement to understand how the reduction in working capital has been affected.

The company has reduced its inventory from its previous levels of 1,300,000 to 800,000.

What I simply cannot understand is that, on the one hand, the organization is planning increased production (as indicated by the purchase of the new plant), and on the other, the physical inventory is actually going down!

It tells me that even though the company now has improved capacity and will be looking at increased levels of production, it is probably going to run out of inventory and will not be able to achieve production targets.

The next item in the working-capital statement is debtors.

These have risen from 450,000 to 500,000.

Debtors increasing is fine, as long as sales also increase.

However, the footnote has told us that sales are constant. Debtors have no business to increase in the absence of an increase in sales!

With constant sales, debtors can go up only in two ways.

Either the old customers are delaying payments, or the organization is being forced to offer longer periods of credit to achieve the same sales value.

Both of these are negative signs.

The next item shows that the bank balance has fallen from 130,000 to 98,000.

When this organization had a bank balance of 130,000 it had a liquidity ratio lower than 1, indicating a need for increased liquid assets. A reduction in bank balance indicates a further deterioration of the liquid situation, as reflected by the worsened quick ratio of 0.56:1.

The next item reveals that the organization has taken a fresh short-term loan in the form of a bank overdraft of 50,000.

This should have actually increased the bank balance. And despite this, the bank balance has reduced.

The reduction in bank balance is even more than it appeared at first to be!

As we can see, creditors have increased from 840,000 to 1.02 million.

Just as in the case of debtors, if the organization has purchased more and thus owed more to creditors, it would be fine. But in this case, sales are constant. Therefore, production and consumption of materials must also be constant, and creditors should be constant too.

I'm afraid not.

Part of this organization's requirement of material has been met from the stocks held as evident from the reduced inventory levels.

Now, if consumption is constant, and part of the requirement is met from existing inventory, it will mean that the current year's purchases must have been lower than before.

If the purchases were lower than before, the company should also owe creditors less than before.

So how do we now explain this contradiction: the company has purchased less but it owes its creditors more?

This can only mean that the old creditors are not being paid.

This is the only way in which an organization can have reduced purchases and still owe more to its vendors.

What can we conclude from all this?

The organization appears to be in serious trouble. Its sales are not increasing. Its collections are inefficient. Its liquidity is so poor that it seems unable to pay its vendors on time.

In this situation, a few questions to the management might be in order.

And the first question is: why was the plant purchased?

Nothing in this example seems to justify the purchase of a plant. But let's give them the benefit of the doubt. Perhaps the organization did indeed need the plant for reasons which are not apparent to a reader of the funds flow statement.

If they were so keen to purchase the plant, they should also have realized that this was a long-term use of funds, and they should have organized a long-term source to finance it.

But apparently, they were so desperate to acquire the plant that when they could not organize long-term resources, they deemed it fit to release money from working capital and divert it for a long-term use, not understanding that this investment would actually result in a further additional requirement of working capital and they would soon be trapped in a vicious cycle.

The next question must pertain to the wisdom of redeeming debentures.

This organization's liquidity is already in such bad shape, due to its inability to increase sales or make timely collection from its debtors, that it is unable to even pay its creditors on time.

Yet, it seems to be paying off its debenture holders, that too at a premium!

The redemption could have been delayed and the premium should certainly not have been paid.

But what really takes the cake is that the management has the temerity to distribute over 65 per cent of its profit among owners as dividends, even though the creditors are daily being denied their due payment!

All said and done, this organization is in dire straits. Unless the management takes immediate steps on a war footing to set things right, it may not be long before the entire organization goes under.

Through this example, I wanted to illustrate how, when you prepare a funds flow statement, you can get an insight into numbers that you would not get merely by looking at a Balance Sheet in isolation.

Part V SUBSISTING TOPICS

CHAPTER 7 Good Finance Management for Nations

To begin with, I have a few questions to ask.

Do the rules of good finance management that apply to a business also apply to the running of a nation?

What does a country's budget look like?

It is a statement that shows the receipts and expenditures of the government for the coming year – where the money will come from and how it plans to spend it.

Expenditures	Budget	Receipts

A budget, by definition, is futuristic. But if the same data is provided for the year gone by, can I then say that would be the country's Balance Sheet?

The answer is yes and no.

What do I mean by that?

A business enterprise makes two statements, a Profit & Loss Account and a Balance Sheet.

Expenses	P&L A/c	Income
Revenue		Earnings

Liabilities	B/S	Assets
Borrowings		Capital

When it earns money, it is reflected on the income side of the Profit & Loss Account, and when it borrows money it appears as a liability on the Balance Sheet.

The budget shows both earnings and borrowings on the receipts' side.

When a business spends money on running its activities (revenue expenditure), these are shown on the expenses' side of the Profit & Loss Account, and when it incurs capital expenditure, those items are shown on the assets' side of the Balance Sheet.

A budget shows both revenue and capital spending on the expenditure side.

So, in a way, a budget is a Profit & Loss Account and a Balance Sheet rolled in one.

Expenditures	Budget	Receipts
Revenue		Earnings
Capital		Borrowings

What is the fundamental difference between a nation's budget and one made by you and I?

Is there a difference?

If we make our personal budget, which side will we prepare first? The receipts' side or the expenditures'?

It will be the receipts' side. We will first figure out how much money we can get and then plan where and how much to spend.

Governments work in reverse. They first decide how much to spend and then they take care of minor details like where the money will come from.

I often get the feeling that there is a completely different set of people planning the expenditures and another group figuring out the receipts, and the two groups are not on talking terms with each other.

If the two groups are not in sync, we can visualize three possibilities.

Let's say the planned expenditure is 100.

Possibility 1: The expected receipts could be 100.

Possibility 2: The expected receipts could amount to 120.

Possibility 3: The expected receipts could be 80.

Expenditures	Budget		Receipts
Revenue	XXX	Earnings	XXX
	XXX		XXX
	XXX		XXX
Capital	XXX	Borrowings	XXX
	100		

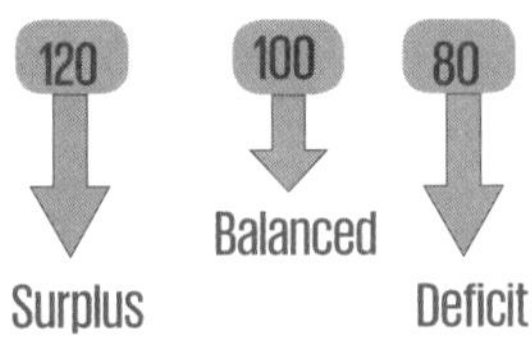

Have you ever seen the first kind of budget? I haven't.

If that possibility occurs, it will then be called a **balanced budget**.

What about the second one? Rarely, if ever.

If it happens, it would be called a **surplus budget**.

Have you ever seen the third type of budget?

We see it year after year after year.

This kind of a budget is called a **deficit budget.**

The first difference between a budget prepared by a government and that prepared by you and I is that governments can have deficits whereas you and I cannot.

What do I mean when I say that you and I cannot have a deficit? Can't we earn 100 and spend 120? We can. We can borrow 20.

But what we cannot do, however, is spend more than what we earn *and* what we borrow.

A government's deficit means that its spending exceeds its earnings plus borrowings.

That you and I cannot do, but a government can.

A government can do that because it also happens to be the owner of the printing press.

When the government discovers that it needs to spend and doesn't have sufficient money to do so, it picks up the phone, calls the nation's printing press and asks it to print more money.

When governments print money to meet expenditure, that phenomenon is called **deficit financing**.

Is there a fallout of deficit financing?

Do you and I pay a price for this tendency of the government to print money and spend?

Is there a fallout of this action?

Yes, there is. Deficit financing is inflationary.

Let's understand in greater detail why deficit financing causes inflation.

Deficit financing, as discussed, is a name given to the printing of money by the government to spend.

Inflation represents either a general increase in prices or a fall in purchasing power.

But the question that begs an answer: the government needed to spend, so it resorted to the creation of money, but why did it result in an increase in the price of the bread at the bakery?

Why does deficit financing cause inflation?

How are prices fixed?

Prices, as we all know, are a result of the function of demand and supply.

When the demand for a commodity goes up, its price will rise, unless supply responds.

When the supply of a commodity goes up, its price will fall, unless demand responds.

For price to go up or down, it is necessary that there is a unilateral increase in either demand or supply.

Imagine that all of us living in a country are earning X amount each month. All of us start working twice as hard, and we begin to earn 2X every month.

What has happened? Everybody's income has doubled. The buying power of the nation has doubled. Will it lead to a price rise'?

The answer is no.

Why not?

How did everybody get two times the amount of money? By working twice as hard. Which means that while the income has doubled, the quantity of goods and services produced and delivered has also doubled. It is non-inflationary.

But when governments print money and spend, there is merely an increase in the quantity of money without a corresponding increase in the quantity of goods and services. More money now chases the same quantity of goods, which results in inflation.

How can inflation be tamed?

This question is easy to answer in theory.

What causes inflation in the first place? The pumping in of money into the economy.

So what will bring inflation down? Sucking the money out of the economy.

Easier said than done. How do you go about doing it?

Inflation occurs when demand exceeds supply. To control inflation, either demand must come down or supply should go up.

In democracies, governments don't control the supply, which is predominantly in private hands.

What the government can control, however, is the demand.

To reduce demand, it is essential that the money in the pockets of the citizens should come down.

For this, governments have two weapons in their arsenal – the fiscal policy and the monetary policy, the former dealing with the taxation policies and the latter controlling the interest rates.

If the government wishes to reduce the money available to spend in order to curb demand, then a fiscal policy measure would be to raise taxes.

However, the reason governments get frantic when inflation rates are high is the fear of losing votes. The voting public perceives unbridled inflation as a failure of the government and a black mark against its functioning. Many governments have been voted out of power due to their inability to rein in inflation.

If the primary driving force to tame inflation was the desire to stay in power and garner more votes, raising of taxes to bring inflation down would be a self-defeating move. While it will no doubt serve the purpose of reducing inflation, it will by no means enhance the government's popularity in the eyes of the electorate.

Most popularity-conscious, voter-pleasing governments would shun this measure.

The only other measure available to the government is the use of the monetary policy.

The central bank will then announce a hike in the interest rates.

When interest rates go up, those who deposit money in banks stand to earn more and those who borrow from banks pay more. Depositing money becomes more attractive and borrowing less.

More people deposit money and less people borrow, resulting in money moving from the pockets of the people into the coffers of the government. The central bank, using tools like the cash reserve ratio and the liquidity ratio, then withdraw the money out of circulation. When money supply in the economy comes down, inflation also comes down.

Coming back to the question I had asked you in the beginning of this chapter.

Do the rules of good finance management that apply to a business also apply to the running of a nation?

In *Romancing the Balance Sheet*, I had given you two rules which ensure sustained growth and prosperity if followed, and extract a price and could even lead to the failure of a business if violated.

The second of those rules was that healthy organizations must ensure that they use long-term funds for long-term purposes and short-term funds for short-term purposes. There is no harm if long-term funds are used for short-term purposes, but they should NEVER use short-term funds for long-term purposes.

In a similar vein, nations must ensure that revenue expenditures are met out of revenue receipts. Capital receipts should be used for capital expenditure. While it is fine to use revenue surplus to meet capital expenditure, a situation to be avoided, at all costs, should be to use capital surplus to meet revenue deficits.

Part V SUBSISTING TOPICS

CHAPTER 8 Stock Market Investing

It is my belief that investing in shares is a national duty. Let's discuss how the learnings from *Romancing the Balance Sheet* and this book can be used to select stocks that can be invested in.

The stock exchange is a market for shares and securities. It is a place where buyers and sellers or their representative brokers meet and enter into deals for the purchase and sale of stock and securities.

It is easier to appreciate the importance of a stock exchange if one visualizes what would happen if there were no such markets. If a person holding shares in a certain company wanted to sell them, he would have to hunt for a buyer informally out of the millions of investors spread all over the country. In the absence of a market, this by itself would be a gigantic task, almost like looking for a needle in a haystack. Having located a buyer, he would then have to negotiate, and, if necessary, bargain to get a fair price. It would be a similar case if one wanted to buy shares. The stock exchange eliminates all these difficulties by providing a common place and having a mechanism for fixing the prices.

How does one go about investing in shares?

It is a cardinal principle of investment that returns can and should be made only steadily.

There is a direct relationship between return and risk. Anybody who has made quick money on the stock exchange must realize that he has undertaken a great deal of risk unknowingly, since a similar practice can result in a disaster in the future.

However, the long-run price behaviour does reflect the general condition of the economy. It is predictable and reflects inherent economic trends.

Investment decisions basically depend upon the following factors:

1. Objective of investment portfolio

It is important to decide at the very outset what one expects from one's investments. For instance, the manager of a provident fund portfolio has to look for security and would prefer to invest in low-risk securities even though the return may not be high. On the other hand, an aggressive investor may be willing to take higher risk in order to have greater capital appreciation.

2. Selection of investment

Once the objective of investment is clear, the next step would be to decide upon the kind of investments to be purchased. Selection of investment would consider the following:

(a) An industry which shows a potential for growth.

(b) Companies where investments (shares or securities) are to be made.

3. Timing of purchase and sale

The timing of buying and selling securities is of crucial importance. Even if one can identify correctly the companies in whose shares the investments are to be made, one may lose money if the timing is inappropriate. The price at which the share is acquired for the portfolio depends entirely on the timing decision.

Company analysis

A company's growth potential can be roughly judged by studying its past performance. However, one should keep in mind that past performance and information are relevant only to the extent that they extend the future trends. An illustrative list of factors that an analyst should take into consideration are as follows:

1. Size and ranking

A rough idea of the size and ranking of the company within the economy, in general, and the industry, in particular, would help the investor in assessing the risk associated with the company. In this regard, the net capital employed, the net profits, the return on investment and the sales figures of the company under consideration may be compared with similar data from the companies in the same industry group. It may also be useful to assess the position of the company in terms of technical know-how and research and development.

2. Growth record

The growth in sales, net income, net capital employed and earnings per share of the company in the past few years should be examined. The following three growth indicators may be particularly looked into: (a) price to earnings ratio, (b) percentage growth rate of earnings per annum and (c) percentage growth rate of net block.

3. Financial analysis

An analysis of its financial statements for the past few years, with the help of certain fundamental ratios, would help the investor understand the financial solvency and liquidity, the efficiency with which the funds are used, the profitability and the operating efficiency of the company.

4. Quality of management

This is an intangible factor with a very important bearing on the share price. Every investor knows that shares of certain business houses command a higher premium than those of similar companies managed by other business houses. This is because of the quality of management, the confidence that investors have in a particular business house, its policy vis-à-vis its relationship with the investors, dividend and financial performance record of other companies in the same group etc. The quality of management has to be seen with reference to the experience, skills and integrity of the persons at the helm of affairs of the company. The policy of the management regarding the relationship with shareholders is an important factor since certain business houses believe in very generous dividends and bonus distributions while others are rather conservative.

Other factors to be kept in mind are the location of the company's manufacturing facilities, the labour–management relations, the pattern of existing stock holdings and the marketability of the shares, the speculative interest in a particular scrip, the specific stock exchange where it is traded and the volume of trading.

Timing your entry and exit

The decision regarding the timing of purchases is particularly difficult because of certain psychological factors.

It is obvious that if one wishes to make any gains one should 'buy cheap and sell dear', that is, buy when the shares are selling at a low price and sell when they are at a high price.

Although this sounds easy, in practice it is very difficult.

An ordinary investor, on the contrary, normally buys when the prices have risen and sells when they have fallen.

When the prices are rising in the share market, everybody joins in the buying spree, since the general environment is one of confidence.

Those who delay buying regret it, as every day prices touch a new high. The ordinary investor joins the buying rush when it is in full steam and, therefore, usually buys the shares at a high price.

When the downturn begins, an atmosphere of despondency pervades.

The ordinary investor gets panicky and as the prices fall every day and reach a new low, he regrets not selling his shares sooner. Ultimately, he sells the shares at a substantial loss, thanking his stars that he has gone out of the market.

This kind of an investment decision is essentially devoid of a sense of timing.

Investments are to be purchased when prices are low and sold when prices are high. This requires swimming against the general current in the market. Hence, there must be an in-built system of timing the purchase or sale of investments so that the psychological factors are ignored and purchases are made when the prices are entering the bull phase and sold when they are entering the bear phase.

If a graph is prepared of the share market prices and fluctuations therein, one would notice that the prices rise for a certain time, say for a year or two, and then fall and remain low for a year or two.

The best way to study the share market prices is to watch the share price index. The BSE Sensex (S&P Bombay Stock Exchange Sensitive Index) and NSE NIFTY 50 (Standard And Poor's CNX Nifty) are two important indices that investors regularly use in India.

The Dow Theory

The Dow theory is probably the most popular theory regarding the behaviour of stock market prices, deriving its name from Charles H. Dow, who established Dow Jones & Company and was the first editor of the *Wall Street Journal*, a leading publication on financial and economic matters in the USA. This theory classifies the movements of prices on the share market into three broad categories: the primary movements, the secondary movements and the daily fluctuations.

The primary movements reflect the trend of the stock market and last from one to three or more years. If one observes the long-range behaviour of the stock market prices, it will be observed that the share markets go into definite phases where the prices consistently rise or fall, that is, the bull and the bear phases.

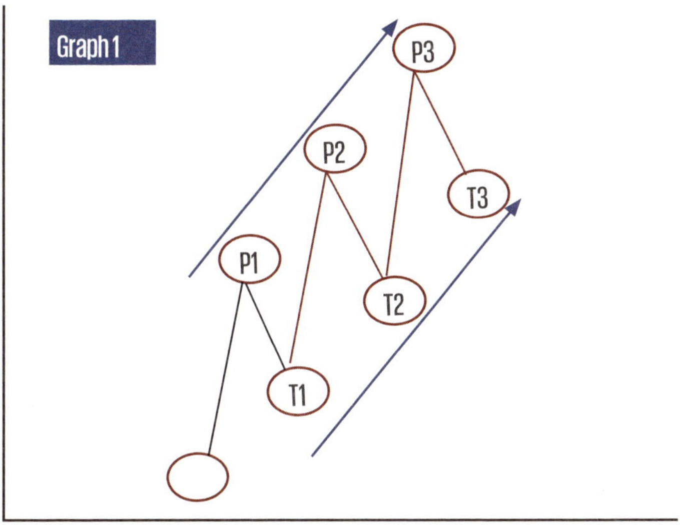

Graph 1 depicts a bull phase where the basic trend is that of a rise in prices. That is, each trough and peak that the prices reach is at a higher level than the earlier one. Thus, P2 is higher than P1 and T2 is higher than T1. Similarly, Graph 2 shows a bear phase where the trend is of a fall in prices.

Even when the market is in a bull phase, after each rise in the prices, there is a fall. Likewise, in a bear phase, one can notice a rise in prices after each fall. Therefore, even though the primary trend is that of a consistent rise and fall in the former and latter cases respectively, there are small movements in the opposite direction also. These movements are known as secondary movements and are shorter in duration. They can last anywhere between three weeks to three months and retrace one-third to two-thirds of the previous advance in the bull market or previous fall in the bear market.

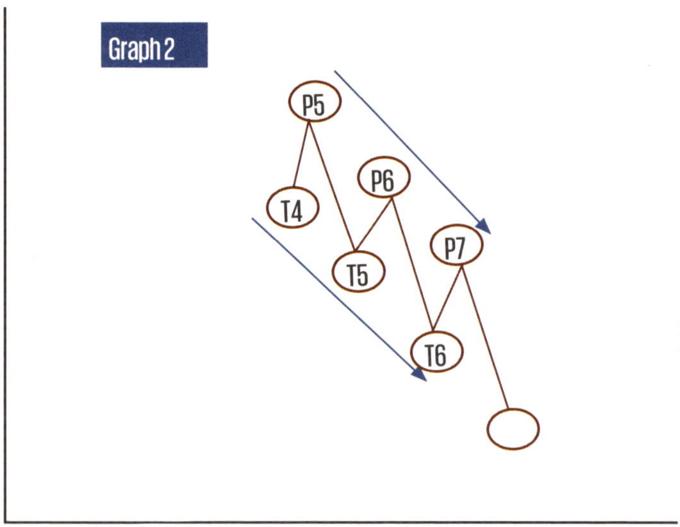

One must learn to distinguish the daily movement from the trend.

Daily movements are irregular fluctuations which occur every day in the market and they are without any definite trend. If the daily share market price index for a few months is plotted on a graph, it will show both upward and downward fluctuations. These fluctuations are the result of speculative factors. An investor should scrupulously keep away from the daily fluctuations of the market.

Timing of investment based on the Dow Theory

In order to time the investments to one's best advantage, one has to be able to identify the bear and bull phases. As indicated above, the primary movements indicate the basic trends in the market. If the cyclical swings in the stock market price indications are successfully higher, the market trend is up and there is a bull phase. On the other hand, if the highs and lows are successfully lower, there is a downward trend and we are in a bear market. Ideally speaking, an investor would like to purchase the shares at a time when the bull phase is just starting and sell when the market is about to enter the bear phase. This means that the investor should be able to identify exactly when the falling or rising trend has begun.

This is known as 'identification of the turn' in the share market prices. Identification of these turns becomes somewhat difficult, because even in a rising market the prices keep falling, and vice versa, as a result of the secondary movements. One has to ascertain whether the rise or fall in the prices is due to a real turn in prices or only due to short-run speculative trends.

The Dow theory identifies the turn in the market prices by seeing whether the successive rise and fall are higher or lower than before.

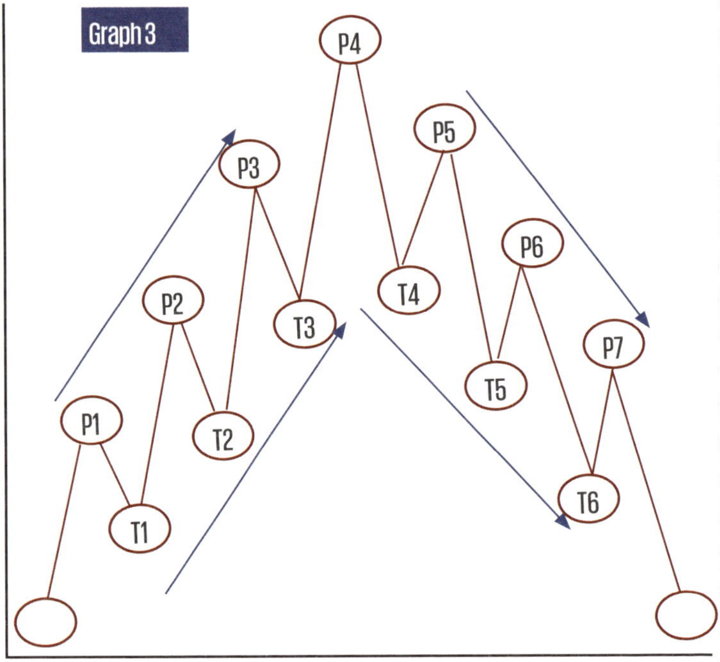

Consider Graph 3. According to the theory, a discerning investor should purchase the investments when the prices are at T2. At this point, he knows that one bull trend has started, since T2 is higher than T1 and P2 is higher than P1. Similarly, when the prices reach P6, he should sell. At this point, he knows that the bearish trend has started, since P6 is lower than P5 and T5 is lower than T4.

Stock market investment strategy

There are many investment strategies to choose from.

Let me share with you one of many.

Let's imagine that, after doing the industry research and the company analysis, you purchased 1,000 shares of a company at the rate of 100 each, making a total investment of 100,000.

Before you even think of the profit that you can make, you must decide the loss you are willing to suffer and put a stop-loss limit.

You may decide that you do not want to lose more than 10 per share. That is, in case the price of this share falls to 90, you will sell and get out. And you will not regret it if the price bounces back.

But since you have done your homework and timed your entry, as discussed above, there is a greater chance that the price will move upward. Let's say, a little later the price increases to 120.

What should you do now?

I want you to remember two phrases that don't exist in the stock market:

1. Maximum profit
2. Minimum loss

If you wait to maximize your profit, you may keep waiting forever. And if you wait to minimize the losses, they may keep mounting for each day of delay.

The time to make a profit or a loss is now.

You had purchased this scrip at 100 and the price has now moved up to 120. What should you do?

Sell a hundred shares at 120.

Why only 100 and not the entire lot?

That is because if the price moves up further, you have more shares to sell. And in case it drops to below 100, you will lose less since the average cost of the remaining 900 shares is now lower than 100. (Remember, this is merely one of many strategies.)

A little later, the price increases to 140.

Sell another 100.

The price goes up to 160.

Sell another 100.

The price now falls to 150.

What should you do?

Buy back what you sold at 160 (provided the original logic applied at the time of buying the initial lot still holds).

Why should you buy it back?

You have sold the stock at 160 and purchased it back at 150. The shares are back with you and you have pocketed a profit of 1,000. What more can you ask for?

At every rise you must sell, at every fall buy back. Unless the price falls to 90, at which point you must sell the entire lot and get out, remember?

In fact, the stop-loss must also be revised once you see the price has gone up first to 120 and then to 140. Why should you be willing to lose anything at all? Maybe you should decide that you will sell the entire lot and exit if the price falls to 110. Above 110, at every rise you must sell and at every fall buy back.

Keep profits open-ended and put a stop-loss.

People often tend to do the reverse. They put a limit on the profit and keep their losses open-ended.

If the scrip that they have invested in appreciates a few percentage points, they sell the entire lot, satisfied with the profit made. And if the price continues rising thereafter, they have no shares left to sell. However, if the price falls below what they have paid for it, they keep hoping and praying that it will bounce back.

If you follow this rule, it will serve you well.

A word of caution: don't let your portfolio become too unwieldy. There are some who don't invest in stocks at all. Others go overboard, having 100 to 150 scrips in the portfolio.

Nobody can be right every time.

If you have a large portfolio, at the best of times, half the scrips that you hold may be looking up and the other half down.

In my opinion, the number of scrips in a portfolio should be in a single digit. This way relatively large sums of money can be invested in each and the amount of investment will justify spending more time on researching the stock well and also monitoring its price movements.

Part V SUBSISTING TOPICS

CHAPTER 9 Income Tax – To Pay or Not to Pay

On the subject of taxation, in general, and income tax, in particular, I have strong views. I thought this book would be incomplete without a discussion on this topic.

What is income tax?

A straightforward answer would be that it is a tax on income. So, to understand income tax we need to understand these two words – tax and income.

What is a tax?

A tax is a levy, a statutory, mandatory payment made to the government.

Now, what is income tax?

When the amount to be paid is a percentage of the income, it is called income tax.

When we pay the government a percentage of the value of goods, it is called value added tax (VAT). When it is a percentage of goods entering the country, it is called customs duty.

When it is a percentage of the value of services rendered, it is a service tax.

We keep paying the government in a variety of ways. Income tax, a percentage of our income, is one of the ways in which we contribute to the running of our country.

The critical word to be understood is 'income'. Unless you know what income is, you will not be able to work out the tax payable on income.

So, what is income? Income from the point of view of income tax is the amount which needs to be declared in the income tax return.

People have several misconceptions when it comes to defining income.

One response is that income is everything that comes in – all the receipts of money. But this is too broad a definition. Many receipts do not constitute income. For example, a loan taken from a bank brings money in but is obviously not income. Also, inheritances are not considered income. Nor are gifts, under certain circumstances.

Another reaction is that income refers to earnings. But unearned receipts, such as winnings from lottery or lucky draws, are also income subject to income tax.

So income is something broader than mere earnings and not as broad as to cover all receipts.

Yet another misconception is that legal earnings are income and illegally obtained money is not.

The truth is that income, for the purposes of income tax, covers almost all the money coming in, barring a few specific exceptions like loans, gifts (in some cases) and inheritances. It does not matter whether it is earned or unearned, legal or illegal, received or accrued.

Should we pay income tax?

It doesn't matter how much it may hurt people to pay taxes, whenever I ask this question, invariably the answer is, 'Yes, of course we should pay taxes.'

What really hurts people is not so much the paying as the misuse of the money paid, or when it goes to the pockets of unscrupulous and corrupt persons. If people were sure that the taxes paid would actually be used for the purpose for which they were collected, more people would pay happily.

Why do we pay taxes?

Taxes are obviously paid so that governments can raise the resources to provide for various facilities meant for you and I. These facilities are those that all of us need, but none of us can provide for ourselves individually.

Even if I don't go into complicated theories of taxation and take some blatant examples of services and amenities that the government provides – roads, street lighting, police, the army – they are of a nature that is neither possible nor affordable for citizens of a country to obtain on their own. I mean, if the government asks each individual to build a road for say a hundred metres outside their respective houses, a majority of the people will not be able to afford it. But how many miles and miles of roads do we use? We use postal services. The police are there to protect us. Without the army guarding our borders, we could become slaves to a marauding and ambitious rogue nation.

So, the logic of income tax, as other taxes, is that all of us use the facilities and hence all of us must pay.

The problem of income tax is all of us use the facilities, but all of us don't pay.

It is not only that all of us don't pay, but all of us can't pay.

And why can't all of us pay? This is because a significant percentage of India's population lives below what is known as the 'poverty line'.

Persons living below the poverty line do not earn enough to have three meals a day.

Even conservative government estimates put the percentage of our population that lives below the poverty line at around 30. Privately, one even hears of a percentage as high as 50.

I have pointed out that the logic of collecting tax is that all of us enjoy the facilities, therefore all of us must pay. Can this 50 per cent afford to pay? Are they even bothered whether the roads have potholes and the street lights are functioning effectively or not. They are struggling merely to survive.

That leaves us with the remaining 50 per cent; the ones that are above the poverty line.

Now, so far as income tax is concerned, the government's stand is that it doesn't want you to pay income tax unless you lead a relatively decent life.

So, those who earn less than the amount needed to live a decent life are not expected to pay any tax at all.

Out of the 50 per cent that are above the poverty line, perhaps 40 per cent earn less than the minimum required to pay income tax.

Now we are left with some 10 per cent of the population that is not only above the poverty line, but has a surplus beyond the minimum, on which they can pay income tax.

And of this 10 per cent, about 60 to 70 per cent are tax evaders.*

(*The percentages used by me to indicate the number of taxpayers and tax evaders are not exact but approximations, and are merely intended to be illustrative.)

Do you see how grave the situation is?

The question I had posed earlier was 'Should we pay taxes?'

My answer is, of course we should.

If for no other reason than as a token of appreciation for occupying the top 2–3 per cent slot of this nation's population; the least we can do is pay our taxes honestly.

I'm not sermonizing. It is the most practical thing to do. **In my opinion, any attempt at evading or even saving taxes is probably more expensive than the payment of tax itself.**

How is evading tax more expensive than paying it?

Let me try and elaborate on this statement.

What we need to understand is that a government's spending is independent of its receipts.

It makes a certain estimate of where the money will come from and where it will be spent.

Let's say the government expected to collect a certain amount of money from income tax. Due to tax evasion on the part of some people, the government collects less than the expected amount.

Do you think that it will not spend or spend less? If tax collection falls short, it will introduce another tax. If direct tax collection is insufficient, it will increase the rate of some indirect tax.

What is the difference between a direct tax and an indirect tax?

Direct taxes are those which, if you have to pay, are collected directly from you by the government, such as income tax.

Indirect taxes are those in which you pay someone else and that person pays it to the government, such as the goods and services tax (GST).

I would any day prefer to pay direct taxes than indirect taxes. This is because direct taxes can be collected according to the ability to pay. Take income tax, for instance. The government can tell one person, your income is too low and there is no need to pay anything, and tell another person, since you are relatively richer, you must pay at a higher rate to make up for those who can't.

However, indirect taxes hit everybody uniformly. If you buy something from a grocery shop and pay 10 as VAT, a beggar wishing to buy the same item will also have to pay 10.

If the government still cannot manage to collect the required amount, it will resort to printing notes, which will result in inflation and reduction in the value of our money.

What I'm trying to say is that eventually it is you and I that have to pay. And if we must pay any which way, then the cheapest and the best way of paying is the original way in which we were supposed to pay.

So, attempting to save or evade taxes is actually a mug's game. One has spent all that time and energy (and maybe lost one's peace of mind in the process too) and in the end gained nothing.

There is an even more sinister dimension to tax evasion.

Let me first show you the brighter side of the picture.

Let's take the case of income tax alone. I receive income and I pay tax on it.

What do I do with this money? I have needs. I am a salaried person and I have been waiting to receive my salary so that I can purchase a shirt for myself. I receive my salary, pay income tax and then go and spend this money on a shirt. This money goes from my pocket to the pocket of the shirt seller. It becomes the shirt seller's income. She pays tax on it. Maybe she has been wanting to buy a pair of shoes. When she spends this money, it becomes the shoe seller's income. The shoe seller pays tax on it. Do you realize each time a rupee merely changes hands it becomes somebody's income and the government gets a share of it?

It has been estimated that out of every rupee that is made, more than 97 paise goes back to the government by way of income tax alone. (Once I was thinking aloud: Why only 97 paise? Why not 5 rupees? And someone pointed out that is probably because by the time 97 paise get collected, the rupee must be worn out and discarded.)

And this is income tax alone. I earn a rupee, I pay income tax. If I use that money to purchase an asset, and if I still own that asset on 31 March, it becomes a part of my wealth on which I must pay wealth tax. And having paid income tax and wealth tax, a little later, in one of my generous moods, if I gift the item to somebody, I am supposed to pay a gift tax. And a little later, if I happen to die, somebody on my behalf is supposed to pay estate duty on the wealth that I leave behind.

Let's first understand the difference between a tax planner and a tax evader.

Those who are supposed to pay tax can broadly be classified into two types: tax planners and tax evaders.

Who is a tax planner? What is a tax planner trying to achieve? A tax planner is a person who is trying to arrange his affairs in such a way that the tax liability gets minimized or eliminated.

What is a tax evader attempting to do? Also trying to minimize or eliminate the tax liability.

The end result of the actions of both is that the government loses tax revenue. But the former is considered to be a respectable citizen and the latter a crook.

Why is that so?

The difference obviously lies in the methods adopted by them.

How does a tax planner save taxes?

The Income Tax Act provides several avenues of saving and investing money that also give tax relief.

How does the tax planner save tax?

By purchasing units in a prescribed mutual fund scheme or by taking a life insurance policy or investing in any of the other avenues prescribed by the Income Tax Act.

How does a tax evader save taxes?

The modus operandi adopted by a tax evader is merely to stay quiet and not reveal the income earned.

In my opinion, the very fact that a tax evader does not pay taxes is a minor crime. (Even the tax planner does not pay taxes in full.) But this minor crime necessarily leads to a major crime.

The cancerous tendencies of black money

The tax evader has to essentially be a very intelligent person, otherwise he will soon get caught.

And how will he get caught?

If this money is used to acquire an expensive property, a luxury car, membership to an exclusive club or other such items, sooner or later he is likely to receive an income tax notice asking to explain the source of these purchases.

Therefore, the avenues of spending for a tax evader get substantially reduced.

When the tax evader realizes that he has the money but is scared to spend it for fear of being detected, this money then finds its way under the tiles in his bathroom.

And here is where the bigger crime begins.

What is the bigger crime?

Both the tax planner and evader have not paid taxes.

But the tax planner is not scared to spend.

The fact that the tax evader did not pay taxes is, as I said earlier, a minor crime.

But the tax evader does not spend to avoid detection. He starts hoarding the money.

And this is a bigger crime. He breaks the chain – the cash is taken out of circulation.

Remember, one person earns money and pays income tax. When he spends, it becomes the recipient's income, who again pays tax. When this person spends, it becomes the next person's income. If that person does not pay tax, I say it is a minor crime. But when that person does not spend (for fear of getting caught), it leads to the bigger crime.

By not spending, the tax evader has not only deprived the nation of the tax that he should have paid but also of the tax that countless people after him would have paid.

And like cancer, it spreads.

The message I am attempting to communicate is that if everyone starts paying taxes honestly, not only would they be better off, but the entire nation, including the tax payers themselves, would stand to benefit abundantly.

Tremendous amounts of energy and time are spent in evading taxes and taking various steps to avoid detection, not to mention the loss of opportunity due to the inability to invest this money further.

If all this time and energy was used instead in more productive ways, the gain would more than offset the cost of tax.

Part VI ANNEXURE

Practice Problem on Making of a Balance Sheet

Make a Profit & Loss Account and Balance Sheet for Atlantic Hotels Ltd from the following information.

Atlantic Hotels Ltd	
Share Capital	500
Loan	500
Building	650
Furniture	125
Advertising	25
Salaries	40
Room Revenue	225
Food & Beverage Revenue	30
F&B Cost (payable)	10
Interest on Loan	@10%
Depreciation:	Building @10%
	Furniture@ 20%

Dr Expenses			Profit & Loss Account Income	Cr
Advertising		25	Room Revenue	225
Salaries		40	F&B Revenue	30
F&B Cost		10		
Interest		50		
Depreciation				
Building	65			
Furniture	25	90		
Profit		40		
		255		255

Cr Liabilities		Balance Sheet Assets				Dr
Share Capital	500	Cash	~~500~~	~~1,000~~	~~350~~	~~225~~
Profit	40	~~200~~	~~160~~	~~385~~	~~415~~	365
Loan	500	Bldg	650	-Dep	65	585
F&B Cost	10	Furn	125	-Dep	25	100
	1,050					1,050

If you wish to learn more about finance management, you can enroll for our
Live & Online Training Sessions
These are highly interactive training sessions covering various topics of Finance Management. These programs are tailor-made to suit your existing business schedules ranging from one and two day seminars to five day workshops.
Dr Anil Lamba
Chartered Accountant, International Corporate Trainer, Financial Literacy Activist and Author of the bestselling book
ROMANCING THE BALANCE SHEET
Call : +91.99 22 351 352
Email : training@lamconschool.com
Website : www.lamconschool.com
LAMCON®
Financial Intelligence for Profitable Growth

ORDER FORM

ANIL LAMBA ON FINANCE | A series of Training Films on Finance Managment

SERIES I
FINANCE FUNDAMENTALS

The two modules in this series are intended to lay a strong foundation for understanding the financial principles discussed in subsequent sessions. Using easy-to-understand, jargon-free language, Dr Lamba introduces the two most important financial statements, and eliminates a number of misconceptions usually associated with commonly-used-yet-often-misinterpreted terms.

	Price	Qty	Amount
MODULE 01 **Understanding Financial Statements** Duration : 55 mins Format : DVD PAL	₹2850 US $ 64.50		
MODULE 02 **What is Profit?** Duration : 60 mins Format : DVD PAL	₹2850 US $ 64.50		

SERIES II
GOOD FINANCE MANAGEMENT

Financial mismanagement is responsible for most business failures the world over. Even the global economic meltdown towards the end of the first decade of this millennium is primarily attributed to financially disastrous decisions.
In this series, Dr Lamba gives his mantra of Good Finance Management and expounds on his Two Golden Rules. Organizations that abide by these rules achieve sustained growth and success and those that violate can suffer serious consequences.

	Price	Qty	Amount
MODULE 01 **A closer look at the Balance Sheet** Duration : 38 mins Format : DVD PAL	₹2850 US $ 64.50		
MODULE 02 **Two Rules of Good Finance Management: An Overview** Duration : 27 mins Format : DVD PAL	₹2850 US $ 64.50		
MODULE 03 **Rule 1 of Good Finance Management: Managing Profitability** Duration : 47 mins Format : DVD PAL	₹2850 US $ 64.50		
MODULE 04 **Rule 2 of Good Finance Management: Managing Cash Flow** Duration : 69 mins Format : DVD PAL	₹2850 US $ 64.50		

SERIES III

MAKING OF A BALANCE SHEET

The usual perception is that it takes years to learn how to make Profit and Loss Accounts and Balance Sheets. Dr Lamba teaches, in a very quick and simple way, how to make these financial statements in, both, the accountants' as well as laypersons' way.

		Price	Qty	Amount
MODULE 01	**Making a Balance Sheet – without any knowledge of accounting** Duration : 44 mins Format: DVD PAL	₹2850 US $ 64.50		
MODULE 02	**Making a Balance Sheet – the accountants' way** Duration : 38 mins Format: DVD PAL	₹2850 US $ 64.50		

SERIES IV

MARGINAL COSTING AND LEVERAGE ANALYSIS

Application of Marginal Costing principles is essential to take financially profitable decisions. In the six modules comprising this series, Dr Lamba explains complicated marginal costing concepts in such an easy and interesting way that will make you wish you had known about it arlier.

		Price	Qty	Amount
MODULE 01	**Trading on Equity** Duration : 47 mins Format : DVD PAL	₹2850 US $ 64.50		
MODULE 02	**Marginal Costing – Break-Even Analysis** Duration : 46 mins Format : DVD PAL	₹2850 US $ 64.50		
MODULE 03	**Cost-Volume-Profit Analysis** Duration : 34 mins Format : DVD PAL	₹2850 US $ 64.50		
MODULE 04	**Marginal Costing – Cases I** Duration : 51 mins Format : DVD PAL	₹2850 US $ 64.50		
MODULE 05	**Marginal Costing – Cases II** Duration : 57 mins Format : DVD PAL	₹2850 US $ 64.50		
MODULE 06	**Leverage Analysis** Duration : 44 mins Format : DVD PAL	₹2850 US $ 64.50		

SERIES V

EVALUATING FINANCIAL PERFORMANCE

In this series two very important tools of evaluating financial statements, Ratio Analysis and Funds Flow Analysis, are explained.

		Price	Qty	Amount
MODULE 01	**Ratio Analysis** Duration : 42 mins Format: DVD PAL	₹2850 US $ 64.50		
MODULE 02	**Ratio Analysis – Cases** Duration : 49 mins Format: DVD PAL	₹2850 US $ 64.50		
MODULE 03	**Funds Flow Analysis – How to read Funds Flow Statements** Duration : 53 mins Format: DVD PAL	₹2850 US $ 64.50		
MODULE 04	**Funds Flow Analysis – How to make Funds Flow Statements** Duration : 43 mins Format: DVD PAL	₹2850 US $ 64.50		

Please note : Shipping & handling charges will be extra

Enclosed is Cheque/Demand Draft No. ______________ dated __________
drawn on ____ bank for
rupees ____
in favour of Lamcon Finance & Management Services Pvt Ltd.

SCAN THE QR CODE

OR DOWNLOAD THIS ORDER FORM ONLINE

www.lamconschool.com/downloads/alf-orderform-2013.pdf

Name : ____

Designation : ____

Company's Name : _____________________________________

Address : ____

________________________ Pin : __________________

Phone No : ____

E-mail : ____

Signature : ____

BANKING DETAILS

ACCOUNT NAME : LAMCON FINANCE & MANAGEMENT SERVICES PVT LTD

ACCOUNT NUMBER : 01482560000665

NAME OF BANK : HDFC Bank Ltd

BRANCH : East Street Branch

ADDRESS : 2418 East Street, Pune 411001, India.

RTGS/NEFT IFSC : HDFC0000148

SWIFT Code : HDFCINBB

Also by Dr Anil Lamba

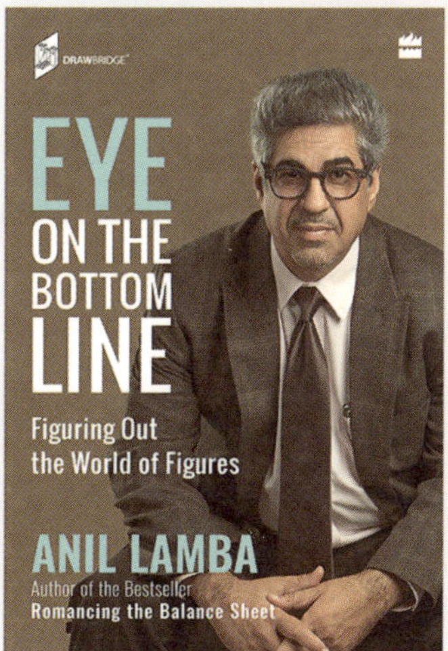